CONTENTS

ESLAM WAHBA

PROMPT ENGINEERING HANDBOOK

Handbook for Prompt Engineering: A Complete Guide and Examples for Prompt Engineering Science from Scratch to Application

CHAPTER 1: INTRODUCTION TO PROMPT ENGINEERING

DEFINE PROMPT ENGINEERING AND ITS IMPORTANCE

Prompt engineering is a specialized subfield within the realm of artificial intelligence (AI) and natural language processing (NLP) that focuses on crafting precise input prompts to elicit desired responses from AI models, particularly language models. As AI systems become increasingly sophisticated, the role of prompt engineering has grown in significance. It serves as the bridge between human intent and machine understanding, enabling more effective and accurate interactions with AI technologies.

The importance of prompt engineering lies in its ability to enhance the performance and reliability of AI systems. By carefully designing prompts, practitioners can improve the quality of responses, reduce ambiguity, and ensure that AI models perform specific tasks with greater accuracy. This is especially crucial in applications where precision and clarity are paramount, such as healthcare, legal analysis, and customer service.

HISTORICAL BACKGROUND AND EVOLUTION

The concept of prompt engineering has its roots in the early days of AI and NLP. Initially, interactions with AI systems were limited to simple commands and queries. However, as language models evolved, the need for more sophisticated and nuanced interactions became apparent. The development of large-scale pre-trained models, such as OpenAI's GPT-3, marked a significant milestone in this evolution.

Early AI systems relied heavily on rule-based approaches, where predefined rules and templates were used to generate responses. These systems were rigid and lacked the ability to handle diverse and complex inputs. The advent of machine learning and neural networks introduced more flexible and adaptive models, capable of learning from large datasets. This shift paved the way for the emergence of prompt engineering as a critical discipline.

In recent years, prompt engineering has become a focal point of research and development. Advances in NLP and AI have led to the creation of more powerful and versatile language models, capable of understanding and generating human-like text. This progress has underscored the need for effective prompt design to harness the full potential of these models.

KEY CONCEPTS AND TERMINOLOGY

To understand prompt engineering, it is essential to familiarize oneself with key concepts and terminology commonly used in the field:

- **Prompt:** A prompt is an input or query provided to an AI model, designed to elicit a specific response. It serves as the starting point for the model's generation process.
- **Token:** Tokens are the basic units of text that models process. They can be words, subwords, or characters, depending on the tokenization method used.
- **Context:** Context refers to the information and background provided within a prompt to guide the model's response. Effective prompts often include relevant context to improve the quality of the generated output.
- **Bias:** Bias in prompt engineering refers to the influence of certain factors on the model's responses, which can lead to skewed or unfair outputs. Addressing bias is a critical aspect of ethical prompt engineering.
- **Fine-tuning:** Fine-tuning involves adjusting a pre-trained model using specific datasets to improve its performance on particular tasks. This process is crucial for optimizing models for prompt engineering applications.
- **Zero-shot, Few-shot, and Many-shot Learning:** These terms describe different levels of training data provided

to the model. Zero-shot learning involves no examples, few-shot learning involves a small number of examples, and many-shot learning involves a larger dataset.

OVERVIEW OF THE BOOK

This book is structured to provide a comprehensive guide to prompt engineering, covering fundamental concepts, advanced techniques, and practical applications. Each chapter builds on the previous one, offering readers a logical progression of topics and insights. The goal is to equip developers, researchers, and NLP enthusiasts with the knowledge and skills needed to excel in the field of prompt engineering.

Chapter 2 delves into the foundations of natural language processing and machine learning, establishing the technical groundwork necessary for understanding prompt engineering. Subsequent chapters explore various types of prompts, design principles, evaluation methods, and ethical considerations.

Advanced topics such as data augmentation, transfer learning, and optimization strategies are covered in detail, providing readers with a deep understanding of cutting-edge techniques. Real-world examples and case studies illustrate successful implementations and highlight practical challenges and solutions.

The book concludes with a forward-looking perspective on the future of prompt engineering, examining emerging trends and potential applications. By the end of this journey, readers will have gained a comprehensive understanding of prompt

engineering and its pivotal role in shaping the future of AI and
NLP.

CHAPTER 2: FOUNDATIONS OF NATURAL LANGUAGE PROCESSING AND MACHINE LEARNING

OVERVIEW OF NLP AND ML

Natural language processing (NLP) and machine learning (ML) are the cornerstones of prompt engineering. NLP is a subfield of AI that focuses on the interaction between computers and human languages. It encompasses a range of tasks, including text analysis, language generation, and machine translation. Machine learning, on the other hand, is a broader discipline that involves developing algorithms and models that can learn from and make predictions based on data.

NLP leverages various techniques from ML to process and understand human language. These techniques enable computers to perform tasks such as sentiment analysis, named entity recognition, and text summarization. At the heart of many NLP applications are language models—complex algorithms designed to generate and understand text.

CORE TECHNIQUES AND ALGORITHMS

Several core techniques and algorithms form the foundation of NLP and ML. Understanding these is crucial for mastering prompt engineering:

- **Tokenization:** The process of breaking down text into smaller units called tokens. This can involve splitting text into words, subwords, or characters, depending on the model's requirements.

- **Embedding:** Embeddings are vector representations of words or tokens that capture their meanings and relationships. Techniques like Word2Vec, GloVe, and BERT are commonly used to generate embeddings.

- **Transformers:** Transformers are a class of models that have revolutionized NLP. They use self-attention mechanisms to process and generate text, enabling models to handle long-range dependencies and capture context effectively.

- **Attention Mechanisms:** Attention mechanisms allow models to focus on specific parts of the input text, enhancing their ability to understand and generate relevant responses.

- **Sequence-to-Sequence Models:** These models, often used in machine translation, generate output sequences based on input sequences. They are foundational in tasks like text summarization and question answering.

RELEVANCE TO PROMPT ENGINEERING

Prompt engineering leverages the principles and techniques of NLP and ML to design effective prompts. By understanding the underlying algorithms and models, practitioners can create prompts that guide AI systems to generate accurate and relevant responses.

For instance, knowledge of tokenization and embeddings helps in crafting prompts that align with the model's understanding of text. Understanding transformers and attention mechanisms enables the design of prompts that provide sufficient context and guidance. Sequence-to-sequence models are particularly relevant for tasks requiring coherent and contextually accurate outputs.

As we delve deeper into the book, each chapter will build on these foundational concepts, exploring how they can be applied to create effective prompts and optimize AI interactions.

CHAPTER 3: TYPES OF PROMPTS AND THEIR APPLICATIONS

NATURAL LANGUAGE PROMPTS

Natural language prompts are the most common type of prompts used in AI and NLP. They involve using everyday language to interact with AI models. These prompts are designed to be intuitive and easily understood by users, making them suitable for a wide range of applications.

For example, a natural language prompt for a language model might be: "Write a summary of the following article." Such prompts are straightforward and leverage the model's ability to understand and generate human-like text. They are used in applications like text generation, question answering, and conversational agents.

SYSTEM-DEFINED PROMPTS

System-defined prompts are more structured and predefined by the system. These prompts often follow specific templates or formats, guiding the model to generate responses in a particular style or structure. They are useful in scenarios where consistency and precision are essential.

An example of a system-defined prompt might be: "Translate the following sentence from English to French: 'The weather is nice today.'" Such prompts ensure that the model produces outputs that adhere to a specific format, making them suitable for tasks like translation and form generation.

CONDITIONAL PROMPTS

Conditional prompts provide additional context or conditions that influence the model's response. These prompts are designed to guide the model based on specific criteria or constraints. They are particularly useful in complex scenarios where the response depends on multiple factors.

For instance, a conditional prompt might be: "Generate a marketing slogan for a new eco-friendly product aimed at young adults." This prompt provides context about the product and the target audience, helping the model generate a more relevant and targeted response.

APPLICATIONS OF DIFFERENT TYPES OF PROMPTS

The choice of prompt type depends on the specific application and desired outcome. Here are some examples of how different types of prompts are applied in various domains:

- **Natural Language Prompts:** Used in chatbots and virtual assistants to facilitate natural and engaging conversations with users.
- **System-Defined Prompts:** Employed in legal document generation to ensure that outputs adhere to standardized formats and legal requirements.
- **Conditional Prompts:** Utilized in creative writing tools to guide the generation of content based on specific themes, genres, or styles.

Understanding the nuances of different prompt types and their applications is crucial for effective prompt engineering. Each type offers unique advantages and challenges, and selecting the right prompt for a given task is key to achieving optimal results.

CHAPTER 4:
DESIGNING
EFFECTIVE PROMPTS

PRINCIPLES OF CLEAR AND SPECIFIC PROMPTS

Designing effective prompts requires a deep understanding of the principles that make prompts clear and specific. A well-crafted prompt should provide unambiguous guidance to the AI model, minimizing the risk of misinterpretation and ensuring that the generated response aligns with the user's intent.

Key principles for designing clear and specific prompts include:

- **Clarity:** Use simple and precise language to convey the desired task. Avoid ambiguous terms and complex sentence structures that might confuse the model.
- **Specificity:** Provide detailed instructions and context to guide the model's response. The more specific the prompt, the better the model can tailor its output to meet the user's needs.
- **Relevance:** Ensure that the prompt includes all necessary information relevant to the task. Irrelevant details can distract the model and lead to suboptimal responses.

CONTEXTUAL INFORMATION AND BACKGROUND

Incorporating contextual information and background is essential for creating effective prompts. Context helps the model understand the nuances of the task and generate more accurate and relevant responses. Providing background information can include:

- **Setting the Scene:** Describe the context or scenario in which the task is to be performed. This helps the model generate responses that are appropriate for the given situation.
- **Providing Examples:** Include examples of desired outputs or similar tasks. Examples serve as references for the model, helping it understand the expected format and content.
- **Specifying Constraints:** Clearly outline any constraints or conditions that should be considered when generating the response. This ensures that the model adheres to specific guidelines or requirements.

TECHNIQUES FOR BALANCING GUIDANCE AND CREATIVITY

Effective prompt engineering requires striking a balance between providing sufficient guidance and allowing for creativity. Overly restrictive prompts can limit the model's ability to generate innovative and diverse responses, while overly vague prompts can lead to irrelevant or unhelpful outputs.

Techniques for balancing guidance and creativity include:

- **Structured Prompts:** Use a combination of open-ended and specific elements in the prompt. For example, "Write a short story about a futuristic city, focusing on the themes of technology and human connection."
- **Iterative Refinement:** Start with a broad prompt and gradually refine it based on the model's initial responses. This iterative approach allows for creative exploration while honing in on the desired outcome.
- **Feedback Loops:** Incorporate feedback mechanisms to evaluate and adjust prompts based on the quality of the generated responses. Continuous feedback helps in fine-tuning prompts to achieve the best results.

By understanding and applying these principles and

techniques, practitioners can design prompts that effectively guide AI models to generate high-quality, relevant, and creative responses.

CHAPTER 5: EVALUATING AND VALIDATING PROMPTS

METRICS FOR ASSESSING PROMPT EFFECTIVENESS

Evaluating the effectiveness of prompts is a critical aspect of prompt engineering. Various metrics can be used to assess how well a prompt performs in eliciting the desired responses from AI models. These metrics include:

- **Accuracy:** Measures the correctness of the generated response in relation to the expected output. High accuracy indicates that the prompt effectively guides the model to produce relevant and precise answers.
- **Relevance:** Assesses how closely the response aligns with the context and intent of the prompt. Relevant responses demonstrate the model's ability to understand and follow the prompt's guidance.
- **Diversity:** Evaluates the variety and creativity of the responses generated by the model. Diverse outputs indicate that the prompt allows for multiple valid interpretations and responses.
- **Coherence:** Examines the logical consistency and clarity of the generated response. Coherent outputs reflect the model's ability to produce structured and comprehensible text.

HUMAN EVALUATION AND FEEDBACK

Human evaluation and feedback are essential components of prompt validation. Involving human evaluators provides insights into the quality and appropriateness of the responses from a user perspective. Techniques for human evaluation include:

- **Rating Systems:** Human evaluators rate the responses based on predefined criteria, such as accuracy, relevance, and coherence. These ratings help identify strengths and weaknesses in the prompts.
- **Comparative Analysis:** Evaluators compare responses generated by different prompts or models to determine which performs better. Comparative analysis provides a deeper understanding of prompt effectiveness.
- **Qualitative Feedback:** Collecting detailed feedback from evaluators helps identify specific issues and areas for improvement. Qualitative insights are valuable for refining prompts and enhancing their performance.

AUTOMATED EVALUATION TECHNIQUES

Automated evaluation techniques complement human evaluation by providing scalable and objective assessments of prompt effectiveness. Common automated methods include:

- **BLEU Score:** Measures the overlap between the generated response and a reference text. It is commonly used in machine translation and text generation tasks.
- **ROUGE Score:** Evaluates the quality of summaries by comparing the overlap of n-grams, word sequences, and word pairs between the generated and reference summaries.
- **Perplexity:** Assesses the likelihood of a given sequence of words in the model's vocabulary. Lower perplexity indicates that the model finds the sequence more probable and thus more aligned with the prompt.
- **Embedding-Based Metrics:** Use embeddings to measure the semantic similarity between the generated response and the reference text. Metrics like BERTScore provide a more nuanced evaluation of textual similarity.

By combining human evaluation with automated techniques, practitioners can obtain a comprehensive understanding of prompt effectiveness. This holistic approach ensures that prompts are thoroughly validated and optimized for real-world applications.

CHAPTER 6: ETHICAL CONSIDERATIONS IN PROMPT ENGINEERING

ADDRESSING BIASES IN PROMPTS

Ethical considerations are paramount in prompt engineering, particularly when it comes to addressing biases. Biases in prompts can lead to unfair, discriminatory, or harmful outputs. To mitigate biases, practitioners should:

- **Analyze Data Sources:** Examine the training data used for the model to identify and address potential biases. Diverse and representative datasets help reduce the risk of biased outputs.
- **Implement Fairness Metrics:** Use fairness metrics to evaluate the equity of responses generated by different prompts. These metrics assess whether the model's outputs are consistent across various demographic groups.
- **Conduct Bias Audits:** Regularly audit prompts and model outputs for biased content. Bias audits involve systematic reviews to identify and rectify biased patterns.

ENSURING FAIRNESS AND INCLUSIVITY

Ensuring fairness and inclusivity in prompt engineering involves creating prompts that consider the needs and perspectives of diverse user groups. Key strategies include:

- **Inclusive Language:** Use language that is respectful and inclusive of all users. Avoid terms or phrases that may be exclusionary or offensive.
- **User-Centered Design:** Involve diverse user groups in the prompt design process to ensure that prompts address their specific needs and concerns.
- **Accessibility Considerations:** Design prompts that are accessible to users with different abilities. This includes using clear and simple language and considering alternative input methods.

CASE STUDIES AND BEST PRACTICES

Real-world case studies illustrate the importance of ethical considerations in prompt engineering. Here are a few examples:

- **Healthcare Applications:** In healthcare, prompts must be designed to avoid biases that could impact patient care. For instance, ensuring that prompts for diagnostic models are based on diverse and representative medical data is crucial for fair and accurate diagnoses.
- **Legal and Financial Domains:** Prompts used in legal and financial applications must be free from biases that could affect decision-making. Implementing fairness metrics and conducting bias audits help maintain the integrity of these systems.
- **Content Moderation:** Prompts used for content moderation on social media platforms must balance the need for free expression with the responsibility to prevent harmful content. Ethical prompt design ensures that moderation systems are fair and transparent.

By following best practices and learning from case studies, practitioners can design prompts that are ethical, fair, and inclusive. This not only enhances the quality of AI interactions but also builds trust and credibility with users.

CHAPTER 7: ADVANCED TECHNIQUES IN PROMPT ENGINEERING

DATA AUGMENTATION AND ACTIVE LEARNING

Advanced techniques such as data augmentation and active learning play a significant role in enhancing prompt engineering. These techniques help improve model performance and robustness by expanding the diversity and quality of training data.

- **Data Augmentation:** Involves generating additional training data by modifying existing data. Techniques like paraphrasing, synonym replacement, and back-translation are commonly used in NLP to create varied prompts and responses.
- **Active Learning:** A method where the model actively selects the most informative examples from a pool of unlabeled data for training. This helps in efficiently improving the model's performance by focusing on challenging or ambiguous prompts.

ENSEMBLE TECHNIQUES AND CONTINUAL LEARNING

Ensemble techniques and continual learning are critical for developing robust and adaptive models in prompt engineering:

- **Ensemble Techniques:** Combine the outputs of multiple models to improve overall performance. Techniques like bagging, boosting, and stacking leverage the strengths of different models to generate more accurate and reliable responses.

- **Continual Learning:** Enables models to adapt and learn from new data over time. This is particularly useful in dynamic environments where prompts and user interactions evolve. Techniques such as incremental learning and transfer learning support continual improvement.

HYPERPARAMETER OPTIMIZATION

Hyperparameter optimization is essential for fine-tuning models to achieve optimal performance in prompt engineering. Key aspects include:

- **Grid Search and Random Search:** Common methods for exploring a range of hyperparameters to identify the best combination for model performance.
- **Bayesian Optimization:** A more efficient approach that uses probabilistic models to guide the search for optimal hyperparameters.
- **Automated Machine Learning (AutoML):** Tools and frameworks that automate the process of hyperparameter tuning, making it accessible to practitioners with varying levels of expertise.

By leveraging these advanced techniques, practitioners can enhance the effectiveness and adaptability of AI models in prompt engineering. These methods contribute to the development of robust, high-performing systems capable of handling diverse and complex tasks.

CHAPTER 8: PROMPT ENGINEERING FOR SPECIFIC DOMAINS

HEALTHCARE AND MEDICAL APPLICATIONS

Prompt engineering in healthcare involves designing prompts that assist in medical diagnosis, treatment recommendations, and patient care. Key considerations include:

- **Precision and Accuracy:** Ensuring that prompts are designed to elicit accurate and reliable medical information. This involves incorporating relevant medical context and terminology.
- **Ethical Considerations:** Addressing ethical issues such as patient privacy, data security, and bias in medical prompts. Ethical prompt design ensures that patient care is fair and unbiased.
- **Use Cases:** Examples of healthcare applications include prompts for diagnostic chatbots, medical record summarization, and personalized treatment recommendations.

FINANCIAL AND LEGAL DOMAINS

Prompt engineering in financial and legal domains requires careful consideration of domain-specific requirements and regulations:

- **Compliance and Accuracy:** Designing prompts that comply with legal and financial regulations. This includes ensuring that prompts generate accurate and legally sound responses.
- **Risk Management:** Addressing potential risks such as financial fraud and legal liability. Prompts must be designed to mitigate these risks through careful wording and context.
- **Use Cases:** Examples include prompts for financial analysis, legal document generation, and compliance monitoring.

MULTILINGUAL AND MULTIMODAL PROMPTS

Prompt engineering for multilingual and multimodal applications involves designing prompts that can handle diverse languages and data types:

- **Multilingual Support:** Creating prompts that are effective across multiple languages. This involves understanding linguistic nuances and cultural differences.
- **Multimodal Integration:** Designing prompts that can process and generate responses based on multiple data types, such as text, images, and audio. This enhances the model's ability to understand and interact with complex inputs.
- **Use Cases:** Examples include multilingual customer support chatbots, multimodal content generation, and cross-language translation.

By focusing on specific domains, practitioners can design prompts that are tailored to the unique requirements and challenges of each field. This enhances the effectiveness and relevance of AI applications across diverse industries.

CHAPTER 9: PRE-TRAINING AND TRANSFER LEARNING

CONCEPTS OF PRE-TRAINING LANGUAGE MODELS

Pre-training is a fundamental process in developing language models for prompt engineering. It involves training models on large-scale datasets to learn general language patterns and structures. Key concepts include:

- **Unsupervised Learning:** Pre-training often uses unsupervised learning, where the model learns from raw text data without explicit labels. This helps the model develop a broad understanding of language.
- **Self-Supervised Learning:** Techniques like masked language modeling and autoregressive modeling are commonly used in pre-training. These methods enable the model to learn contextual relationships and generate coherent text.

BENEFITS OF TRANSFER LEARNING

Transfer learning leverages pre-trained models for specific tasks by fine-tuning them on smaller, task-specific datasets. Benefits include:

- **Reduced Training Time:** Pre-trained models require less time and computational resources for fine-tuning compared to training from scratch.
- **Improved Performance:** Transfer learning enhances model performance by building on the general language knowledge acquired during pre-training.
- **Adaptability:** Pre-trained models can be adapted to various tasks and domains with minimal additional training.

TECHNIQUES FOR DOMAIN ADAPTATION

Domain adaptation involves fine-tuning pre-trained models to perform well in specific domains. Techniques include:

- **Fine-Tuning:** Adjusting the pre-trained model's parameters using domain-specific data. This helps the model adapt to the nuances and requirements of the target domain.
- **Domain-Specific Embeddings:** Creating embeddings that capture the unique characteristics of the target domain. This enhances the model's ability to understand and generate domain-specific language.
- **Data Augmentation:** Using data augmentation techniques to generate diverse and representative domain-specific training data. This helps the model generalize better to the target domain.

By understanding and applying these techniques, practitioners can effectively leverage pre-training and transfer learning to develop high-performing models for prompt engineering. This approach enables the creation of versatile and adaptable AI systems capable of handling a wide range of tasks and domains.

CHAPTER 10: OPTIMIZING PROMPT-BASED MODELS

STRATEGIES FOR FINE-TUNING AND OPTIMIZATION

Optimizing prompt-based models involves fine-tuning and adjusting various parameters to achieve the best performance. Strategies include:

- **Learning Rate Adjustment:** Experimenting with different learning rates to find the optimal balance between convergence speed and model stability.
- **Regularization Techniques:** Implementing regularization methods such as dropout and weight decay to prevent overfitting and improve generalization.
- **Batch Size Optimization:** Adjusting batch sizes to balance training speed and model performance. Larger batches can lead to faster training but may require more computational resources.

REINFORCEMENT LEARNING AND POLICY OPTIMIZATION

Reinforcement learning (RL) and policy optimization are advanced techniques for optimizing prompt-based models:

- **Reinforcement Learning:** Involves training models through a reward-based system, where the model learns to generate responses that maximize cumulative rewards. RL is useful for tasks requiring long-term planning and decision-making.
- **Policy Optimization:** Techniques such as Proximal Policy Optimization (PPO) and Trust Region Policy Optimization (TRPO) are used to improve the model's response generation policies. These methods help refine the model's behavior and performance.

CONTINUOUS MONITORING AND FEEDBACK

Continuous monitoring and feedback are essential for maintaining and improving the performance of prompt-based models:

- **Performance Monitoring:** Regularly tracking key performance metrics such as accuracy, relevance, and coherence. Monitoring helps identify areas for improvement and ensures that the model meets desired standards.
- **Feedback Loops:** Incorporating user feedback to refine prompts and model responses. Feedback loops enable continuous improvement by addressing issues and adapting to user needs.
- **Automated Monitoring Systems:** Implementing automated systems to monitor model performance in real-time. These systems can detect anomalies, track trends, and provide actionable insights for optimization.

By employing these strategies, practitioners can optimize prompt-based models to deliver high-quality, reliable, and efficient responses. Continuous monitoring and feedback ensure that models remain effective and adaptable to changing requirements and user expectations.

CHAPTER 11: CASE STUDIES IN PROMPT ENGINEERING

SUCCESSFUL IMPLEMENTATIONS IN VARIOUS INDUSTRIES

Case studies provide valuable insights into the successful implementation of prompt engineering across different industries. Here are a few examples:

- **Healthcare:** A diagnostic chatbot uses carefully designed prompts to collect patient symptoms and provide preliminary diagnoses. The chatbot's effectiveness is enhanced by prompts that elicit detailed and accurate patient information.
- **Customer Service:** An AI-powered customer support system uses natural language prompts to handle common queries and issues. The system's success is attributed to prompts that guide users to provide relevant details, enabling accurate and timely responses.
- **Content Creation:** A content generation tool uses conditional prompts to create tailored marketing materials. The tool's prompts include specific guidelines on tone, style, and target audience, resulting in high-quality and relevant content.

CHALLENGES AND SOLUTIONS

Prompt engineering presents various challenges, which can be addressed through innovative solutions:

- **Ambiguity:** Ambiguous prompts can lead to inconsistent responses. Solutions include refining prompt clarity, providing context, and using examples to guide the model.
- **Bias:** Bias in prompts can result in unfair or discriminatory outputs. Solutions involve analyzing training data, implementing fairness metrics, and conducting bias audits.
- **Complexity:** Complex tasks may require sophisticated prompts to elicit accurate responses. Solutions include using structured prompts, iterative refinement, and incorporating feedback loops.

LESSONS LEARNED AND FUTURE DIRECTIONS

Case studies offer valuable lessons for prompt engineering, highlighting best practices and areas for future development:

- **Iterative Design:** Successful prompt engineering often involves iterative design and testing. Continuous refinement based on feedback and performance metrics is key to achieving optimal results.
- **Ethical Considerations:** Addressing ethical issues such as bias and fairness is crucial for building trustworthy AI systems. Best practices include using diverse data sources, implementing fairness metrics, and involving diverse user groups in the design process.
- **Innovation:** The future of prompt engineering lies in innovative techniques and approaches. Emerging trends such as multimodal prompts, interactive AI systems, and domain-specific adaptations offer exciting opportunities for advancement.

By learning from successful implementations and addressing challenges, practitioners can enhance their prompt engineering practices and contribute to the ongoing development of the field.

CHAPTER 12: THE FUTURE OF PROMPT ENGINEERING

EMERGING TRENDS AND TECHNOLOGIES

The field of prompt engineering is rapidly evolving, with several emerging trends and technologies shaping its future:

- **Multimodal Prompting:** Combining text, images, audio, and other modalities in prompts to enhance the model's understanding and generation capabilities. This trend opens up new possibilities for more interactive and versatile AI systems.
- **Interactive AI:** Developing AI systems that can engage in dynamic and interactive dialogues with users. Interactive prompting allows for more natural and flexible interactions, enabling AI to handle complex tasks and scenarios.
- **Personalized Prompting:** Creating personalized prompts that adapt to individual user preferences and contexts. Personalized prompting enhances user experience by delivering more relevant and tailored responses.

POTENTIAL APPLICATIONS AND IMPACT

The future of prompt engineering holds significant potential for diverse applications and impact across various domains:

- **Education:** Personalized and adaptive learning systems that use prompts to guide students through educational content. These systems can provide customized feedback and support, enhancing learning outcomes.
- **Healthcare:** Advanced diagnostic and treatment recommendation systems that use multimodal prompts to gather comprehensive patient information. These systems can improve the accuracy and efficiency of medical care.
- **Business:** Intelligent customer service and support systems that use interactive and personalized prompts to handle a wide range of queries and issues. These systems can enhance customer satisfaction and operational efficiency.

ONGOING RESEARCH AND DEVELOPMENT

Ongoing research and development efforts are focused on addressing current challenges and exploring new frontiers in prompt engineering:

- **Bias Mitigation:** Developing advanced techniques to identify and mitigate biases in prompts and model outputs. Research in fairness and ethics is critical for building trustworthy AI systems.
- **Human-AI Collaboration:** Exploring ways to enhance collaboration between humans and AI through improved prompting techniques. This includes developing systems that can understand and respond to complex human instructions and feedback.
- **Scalability:** Investigating methods to scale prompt engineering practices to handle large-scale and diverse applications. This includes optimizing model performance, enhancing data processing capabilities, and improving prompt design tools.

The future of prompt engineering is bright, with exciting opportunities for innovation and impact. By staying informed about emerging trends and engaging in ongoing research, practitioners can contribute to the advancement of the field and the development of more effective and ethical AI systems.

CHAPTERS 13-25: [ADDITIONAL RELEVANT CHAPTERS]

For the remaining chapters, we will include additional relevant topics such as practical examples, coding implementations, advanced strategies, and specific use cases in various industries. Each chapter will provide unique insights and value, building on the concepts introduced previously and offering comprehensive guidance for prompt engineering practitioners.

By following this structured and detailed approach, we aim to create a definitive educational and practical guide for developers, researchers, and NLP enthusiasts. The goal is to equip readers with the knowledge and skills needed to excel in the field of prompt engineering and leverage its full potential for real-world applications.

CHAPTER 13: PRACTICAL EXAMPLES OF PROMPT ENGINEERING

INTRODUCTION TO PRACTICAL EXAMPLES

In this chapter, we will explore practical examples of prompt engineering across various applications. By examining real-world scenarios, we aim to provide concrete insights into the effective design and implementation of prompts. Each example will illustrate key principles and techniques, offering valuable lessons for practitioners.

EXAMPLE 1: CUSTOMER SUPPORT CHATBOT

Scenario: A company wants to deploy a customer support chatbot to handle common inquiries and issues efficiently.

Objective: Design prompts that guide the chatbot to provide accurate and helpful responses to user queries.

Steps:

1. **Identify Common Queries:**
   o   Compile a list of frequently asked questions (FAQs) based on customer support data.
   o   Examples include questions about product features, order status, return policies, and technical support.
2. **Design Clear and Specific Prompts:**
   o   For product features: "Can you provide details about [Product Name]?"
   o   For order status: "What is the current status of order #[Order Number]?"
   o   For return policies: "What is the return policy for [Product Category]?"
   o   For technical support: "I need help with [Issue Description] regarding [Product Name]."
3. **Incorporate Context and Examples:**
   o   Provide the chatbot with context about the company's products, policies, and support processes.

○ Include example responses to guide the chatbot's outputs.

4. **Evaluate and Refine Prompts:**

○ Test the chatbot with sample queries to assess the accuracy and relevance of responses.

○ Collect user feedback to identify areas for improvement.

○ Refine prompts based on evaluation results.

Outcome: The chatbot effectively handles common inquiries, reducing the workload on human support agents and improving customer satisfaction.

EXAMPLE 2: MEDICAL DIAGNOSIS ASSISTANT

Scenario: A healthcare provider seeks to implement an AI-powered assistant to support medical diagnosis.

Objective: Design prompts that help the assistant gather comprehensive patient information and provide accurate preliminary diagnoses.

Steps:

1. **Identify Key Diagnostic Questions:**
   - Develop a list of diagnostic questions based on common symptoms and medical conditions.
   - Examples include questions about symptoms, medical history, and lifestyle factors.

2. **Design Detailed and Contextual Prompts:**
   - For symptom inquiry: "Please describe any symptoms you are experiencing, including their duration and severity."
   - For medical history: "Do you have any pre-existing medical conditions or recent surgeries?"
   - For lifestyle factors: "Can you provide information about your diet, exercise routine, and any medications you are taking?"

3. **Integrate Medical Context:**
   - Provide the assistant with medical context and

terminology to ensure accurate understanding and response generation.

o   Include examples of diagnostic scenarios and appropriate responses.

4. **Evaluate and Validate Prompts:**

o   Conduct trials with sample patient data to evaluate the assistant's diagnostic accuracy.

o   Seek feedback from medical professionals to validate the quality and relevance of prompts.

Outcome: The medical diagnosis assistant accurately collects patient information and provides reliable preliminary diagnoses, enhancing the efficiency and accuracy of medical consultations.

EXAMPLE 3: CONTENT GENERATION TOOL

Scenario: A marketing team wants to use an AI tool to generate engaging content for various campaigns.

Objective: Design prompts that guide the tool to produce high-quality content tailored to specific marketing goals and audiences.

Steps:

1. **Define Content Goals:**
   o   Identify the objectives for different types of content, such as blog posts, social media updates, and email newsletters.
   o   Examples include promoting a new product, increasing brand awareness, and engaging with followers.

2. **Design Targeted Prompts:**
   o   For blog posts: "Write a blog post about the benefits of [Product/Service], highlighting key features and customer testimonials."
   o   For social media updates: "Create a social media post announcing our new product launch, including a call-to-action for followers to learn more."
   o   For email newsletters: "Draft an email newsletter featuring our latest product updates, upcoming

events, and special offers."

3. **Provide Context and Examples:**

o   Include background information about the brand, target audience, and previous successful content.

o   Provide example content to illustrate the desired tone, style, and structure.

4. **Evaluate and Optimize Prompts:**

o   Review the generated content for quality, relevance, and alignment with marketing goals.

o   Gather feedback from the marketing team to identify areas for improvement.

o   Refine prompts based on evaluation results.

Outcome: The content generation tool produces engaging and targeted content that supports the marketing team's objectives, increasing brand visibility and customer engagement.

LESSONS LEARNED FROM PRACTICAL EXAMPLES

These practical examples highlight several key lessons for effective prompt engineering:

- **Clarity and Specificity:** Clear and specific prompts lead to more accurate and relevant responses.
- **Context and Background:** Providing contextual information enhances the model's understanding and output quality.
- **Evaluation and Feedback:** Continuous evaluation and refinement of prompts are essential for optimizing performance.
- **Domain-Specific Adaptation:** Tailoring prompts to specific domains and use cases improves the effectiveness of AI applications.

By applying these lessons, practitioners can design prompts that effectively guide AI models to generate high-quality and relevant responses across various applications.

CHAPTER 14: CODING IMPLEMENTATIONS FOR PROMPT ENGINEERING

INTRODUCTION TO CODING IMPLEMENTATIONS

In this chapter, we will delve into the practical aspects of implementing prompt engineering techniques using code. We will explore coding examples and frameworks that facilitate the design, evaluation, and optimization of prompts. These implementations will provide a hands-on approach to mastering prompt engineering.

SETTING UP THE ENVIRONMENT

Before diving into coding examples, it's essential to set up the necessary environment. This includes installing relevant libraries and frameworks commonly used in NLP and prompt engineering.

Required Libraries:

- transformers: A library by Hugging Face for working with transformer models.
- torch: A deep learning framework for building and training models.
- nltk: A library for natural language processing tasks.
- pandas: A library for data manipulation and analysis.

Installation:

bash
  code
```
pip install transformers torch nltk pandas
```

EXAMPLE 1: DESIGNING PROMPTS FOR A LANGUAGE MODEL

Objective: Implement a basic example of designing and using prompts with a pre-trained language model.

Steps:

1. **Import Libraries:**

python
    code

```python
from transformers import GPT2Tokenizer, GPT2LMHeadModel

# Load pre-trained GPT-2 model and tokenizer
tokenizer = GPT2Tokenizer.from_pretrained('gpt2')
model = GPT2LMHeadModel.from_pretrained('gpt2')
```

2. **Design a Prompt:**

python
    code

```python
prompt_text = "Write a short story about a futuristic city where technology and nature coexist."
```

3. **Tokenize the Prompt:**

python
 code

```
input_ids           =           tokenizer.encode(prompt_text,
return_tensors='pt')
```

4. Generate a Response:

python
 code

```
output   =   model.generate(input_ids,   max_length=100,
num_return_sequences=1)
generated_text          =          tokenizer.decode(output[0],
skip_special_tokens=True)

print(generated_text)
```

Outcome: The model generates a short story based on the provided prompt, demonstrating the practical use of prompt engineering with a pre-trained language model.

EXAMPLE 2: EVALUATING PROMPT EFFECTIVENESS

Objective: Implement a method to evaluate the effectiveness of different prompts using automated metrics.

Steps:

1. Define Multiple Prompts:

python
code
```
prompts = [
    "Describe the benefits of exercise.",
    "Explain the advantages of regular physical activity.",
    "What are the health benefits of working out regularly?"
]
```

2. Generate Responses for Each Prompt:

python
code
```
responses = []
for prompt in prompts:
    input_ids = tokenizer.encode(prompt, return_tensors='pt')
    output = model.generate(input_ids, max_length=50, num_return_sequences=1)
```

```
response            =            tokenizer.decode(output[0],
skip_special_tokens=True)
    responses.append(response)
```

3. Evaluate Responses Using Automated Metrics:

python
```
code
from nltk.translate.bleu_score import sentence_bleu
```

# Reference response for comparison
reference = "Regular exercise improves overall health, enhances cardiovascular fitness, and boosts mental well-being."

Calculate BLEU scores for each response
bleu_scores   =   [sentence_bleu([reference.split()],
response.split()) for response in responses]

for i, score in enumerate(bleu_scores):
    print(f"Prompt {i+1} BLEU Score: {score:.4f}")

Outcome: The BLEU scores provide a quantitative measure of the effectiveness of each prompt, allowing for objective comparison and refinement.

EXAMPLE 3: OPTIMIZING PROMPTS WITH HYPERPARAMETER TUNING

Objective: Implement hyperparameter tuning to optimize the performance of prompts using grid search.

Steps:

1. **Define Hyperparameters and Prompts:**

python
   code
```
hyperparameters = {
    'max_length': [50, 100, 150],
    'num_return_sequences': [1, 2, 3]
}
prompt = "Summarize the impact of climate change on global ecosystems."
```

2. **Perform Grid Search:**

python
   code
```
from itertools import product
```

ESLAM WAHBA

```
best_score = 0
best_params = None
for       max_length,       num_return_sequences       in
product(hyperparameters['max_length'],
hyperparameters['num_return_sequences']):
    input_ids = tokenizer.encode(prompt, return_tensors='pt')
    output              =              model.generate(input_ids,
max_length=max_length,
num_return_sequences=num_return_sequences)
    response             =             tokenizer.decode(output[0],
skip_special_tokens=True)

    # Assume we have a function to evaluate the response, e.g.,
a custom metric
    score = evaluate_response(response)

    if score > best_score:
        best_score = score
        best_params       =       {'max_length':       max_length,
'num_return_sequences': num_return_sequences}

print(f"Best    Parameters:    {best_params},    Best    Score:
{best_score}")
```

Outcome: The grid search identifies the optimal hyperparameters for generating the best possible response to the prompt, demonstrating the practical application of hyperparameter tuning in prompt engineering.

CONCLUSION

This chapter provided practical coding examples for implementing prompt engineering techniques using pre-trained language models. By following these examples, practitioners can gain hands-on experience in designing, evaluating, and optimizing prompts, enhancing their ability to create effective and high-quality AI interactions.

CHAPTER 15: ADVANCED STRATEGIES FOR PROMPT ENGINEERING

INTRODUCTION TO ADVANCED STRATEGIES

In this chapter, we will explore advanced strategies for prompt engineering, focusing on techniques that enhance the effectiveness and adaptability of AI models. These strategies include multi-turn prompting, interactive dialogue systems, and leveraging external knowledge bases. By mastering these advanced approaches, practitioners can push the boundaries of what is possible with prompt engineering.

MULTI-TURN PROMPTING

Concept: Multi-turn prompting involves designing prompts that guide a sequence of interactions or dialogues with the AI model. This approach is particularly useful for complex tasks requiring multiple steps or iterative refinement.

Implementation:

1. Define Initial and Follow-Up Prompts:

python
```
code
initial_prompt = "Explain the process of photosynthesis."
follow_up_prompts = [
    "What are the main stages of photosynthesis?",
    "Can you describe the role of chlorophyll in photosynthesis?",
    "How does sunlight contribute to the photosynthesis process?"
]
```

2. Generate Responses for Each Turn:

python
```
code
responses = []
input_ids = tokenizer.encode(initial_prompt, return_tensors='pt')
output = model.generate(input_ids, max_length=50, num_return_sequences=1)
```

```
initial_response                =               tokenizer.decode(output[0],
skip_special_tokens=True)
responses.append(initial_response)

for prompt in follow_up_prompts:
    input_ids = tokenizer.encode(prompt, return_tensors='pt')
    output    =    model.generate(input_ids,    max_length=50,
num_return_sequences=1)
    response               =               tokenizer.decode(output[0],
skip_special_tokens=True)
    responses.append(response)

for i, response in enumerate(responses):
    print(f"Turn {i+1} Response: {response}")
```

Outcome: Multi-turn prompting enables the model to engage in a coherent and informative dialogue, providing detailed and step-by-step explanations.

INTERACTIVE DIALOGUE SYSTEMS

Concept: Interactive dialogue systems use dynamic and adaptive prompts to create more natural and engaging interactions with users. These systems can handle complex conversations, adapt to user inputs, and provide personalized responses.

Implementation:

1. **Design Dynamic Prompts:**

python
code
```python
def generate_dynamic_prompt(user_input):
    if "photosynthesis" in user_input:
        return "Explain the process of photosynthesis in detail."
    elif "chlorophyll" in user_input:
        return "Describe the role of chlorophyll in photosynthesis."
    else:
        return "I'm sorry, I don't understand. Can you please provide more context?"
```

2. **Interactive Dialogue Loop:**

python
code
```python
user_inputs = [
    "Tell me about photosynthesis.",
    "What is the role of chlorophyll?",
```

"How does sunlight affect the process?"
]

```
for user_input in user_inputs:
    prompt = generate_dynamic_prompt(user_input)
    input_ids = tokenizer.encode(prompt, return_tensors='pt')
    output    =    model.generate(input_ids,    max_length=50,
num_return_sequences=1)
    response              =              tokenizer.decode(output[0],
skip_special_tokens=True)
    print(f"User    Input:    {user_input}\nModel    Response:
{response}\n")
```

Outcome: The interactive dialogue system provides relevant and context-aware responses, enhancing user engagement and satisfaction.

LEVERAGING EXTERNAL KNOWLEDGE BASES

Concept: Integrating external knowledge bases with prompt engineering enhances the model's ability to provide accurate and comprehensive responses by accessing up-to-date information.

Implementation:

1. Integrate Knowledge Base:

python
code

```python
knowledge_base = {
    "photosynthesis": "Photosynthesis is the process by which green plants and some other organisms use sunlight to synthesize foods with the help of chlorophyll and carbon dioxide.",
    "chlorophyll": "Chlorophyll is a green pigment found in the chloroplasts of plants, which is essential for photosynthesis."
}

def generate_knowledge_based_prompt(topic):
    if topic in knowledge_base:
        return knowledge_base[topic]
    else:
        return "I'm sorry, I don't have information on that topic."
```

2. Generate Knowledge-Based Responses:

python
code

```
topics = ["photosynthesis", "chlorophyll", "cell division"]
for topic in topics:
    prompt = generate_knowledge_based_prompt(topic)
    input_ids = tokenizer.encode(prompt, return_tensors='pt')
    output = model.generate(input_ids, max_length=50,
num_return_sequences=1)
    response = tokenizer.decode(output[0],
skip_special_tokens=True)
    print(f"Topic: {topic}\nModel Response: {response}\n")
```

Outcome: By leveraging external knowledge bases, the model provides accurate and detailed responses, enhancing its utility for educational and informational purposes.

CONCLUSION

Advanced strategies for prompt engineering, such as multi-turn prompting, interactive dialogue systems, and leveraging external knowledge bases, significantly enhance the capabilities and effectiveness of AI models. These techniques enable practitioners to create more dynamic, informative, and engaging AI interactions, pushing the boundaries of what is possible with prompt engineering.

In the following chapters, we will continue to explore additional topics and advanced strategies, providing comprehensive guidance for practitioners to master the art and science of prompt engineering. Each chapter will build on the concepts introduced previously, offering new insights and practical applications to further enhance the effectiveness of AI models.

CHAPTER 16: ADDRESSING CHALLENGES IN PROMPT ENGINEERING

INTRODUCTION
TO CHALLENGES

Prompt engineering, while powerful, comes with its own set of challenges. These challenges can impact the effectiveness, reliability, and ethical considerations of AI systems. In this chapter, we will address common challenges in prompt engineering and provide strategies to overcome them. By understanding and tackling these issues, practitioners can enhance the robustness and fairness of their AI models.

AMBIGUITY IN PROMPTS

Challenge: Ambiguous prompts can lead to inconsistent or irrelevant responses from AI models. Ambiguity arises from unclear wording, lack of context, or multiple possible interpretations.

Strategies to Overcome Ambiguity:

1. **Clarity in Language:**
   o   Use precise and unambiguous language in prompts.
   o   Avoid jargon and complex sentence structures that might confuse the model.
2. **Context Provision:**
   o   Provide sufficient context to guide the model's understanding.
   o   Include background information and examples to clarify the prompt.
3. **Iterative Refinement:**
   o   Test prompts with sample queries to identify ambiguous areas.
   o   Refine prompts based on feedback and model performance.

Example Implementation:

```python
code
prompt_ambiguous = "Describe the bank's role."
prompt_clear = "Describe the role of a commercial bank
```

in financial transactions, including lending and deposit services."

```
input_ids_ambiguous = tokenizer.encode(prompt_ambiguous,
return_tensors='pt')
input_ids_clear        =        tokenizer.encode(prompt_clear,
return_tensors='pt')

output_ambiguous = model.generate(input_ids_ambiguous,
max_length=50, num_return_sequences=1)
output_clear        =        model.generate(input_ids_clear,
max_length=50, num_return_sequences=1)

response_ambiguous                                        =
tokenizer.decode(output_ambiguous[0],
skip_special_tokens=True)
response_clear        =        tokenizer.decode(output_clear[0],
skip_special_tokens=True)

print(f"Ambiguous        Prompt        Response:
{response_ambiguous}")
print(f"Clear Prompt Response: {response_clear}")
```

BIAS IN PROMPTS AND MODELS

Challenge: Biases in prompts and models can lead to unfair or discriminatory outputs, affecting the trustworthiness and ethical integrity of AI systems.

Strategies to Address Bias:

1. **Diverse Data Sources:**
   o   Use diverse and representative datasets for training models.
   o   Ensure that the data includes various demographic groups and perspectives.
2. **Bias Detection and Mitigation:**
   o   Implement tools and techniques to detect biases in prompts and model outputs.
   o   Use fairness metrics and bias audits to identify and address biased patterns.
3. **Inclusive Language:**
   o   Design prompts using inclusive language that respects all user groups.
   o   Avoid stereotypes and discriminatory terms.

Example Implementation:

python
  code
```
def detect_bias(prompt, model):
    input_ids = tokenizer.encode(prompt, return_tensors='pt')
    output    =    model.generate(input_ids,    max_length=50,
```

```python
num_return_sequences=1)
    response = tokenizer.decode(output[0],
skip_special_tokens=True)

    # Simple bias detection example
    bias_keywords = ["race", "gender", "ethnicity"]
    if any(keyword in response.lower() for keyword in
bias_keywords):
        print(f"Potential Bias Detected in Response: {response}")
    else:
        print(f"Response: {response}")

prompt_bias = "Describe the characteristics of a typical leader."
detect_bias(prompt_bias, model)
```

HANDLING COMPLEX TASKS

Challenge: Complex tasks requiring detailed and structured responses can be challenging for AI models, especially when prompts are not sufficiently detailed.

Strategies to Handle Complex Tasks:

1. **Structured Prompts:**
   o   Break down complex tasks into smaller, manageable sub-tasks.
   o   Use structured prompts that guide the model step-by-step.
2. **Multi-Turn Dialogues:**
   o   Employ multi-turn dialogues to iteratively gather information and refine responses.
   o   Use follow-up prompts to address different aspects of the task.
3. **Contextual Guidance:**
   o   Provide detailed context and examples to help the model understand the task requirements.
   o   Include specific instructions and constraints in the prompts.

Example Implementation:

python
   code
```
prompt_complex = "Explain the process of setting up a business from scratch."
```

```python
# Structured Prompts
prompt_step1 = "Describe the initial steps in setting up a business, including market research and business planning."
prompt_step2 = "Explain the legal requirements for setting up a business, such as registration and licensing."
prompt_step3 = "Detail the financial aspects of setting up a business, including funding and budgeting."

# Generate Responses for Each Step
input_ids_step1 = tokenizer.encode(prompt_step1, return_tensors='pt')
input_ids_step2 = tokenizer.encode(prompt_step2, return_tensors='pt')
input_ids_step3 = tokenizer.encode(prompt_step3, return_tensors='pt')

output_step1 = model.generate(input_ids_step1, max_length=100, num_return_sequences=1)
output_step2 = model.generate(input_ids_step2, max_length=100, num_return_sequences=1)
output_step3 = model.generate(input_ids_step3, max_length=100, num_return_sequences=1)

response_step1 = tokenizer.decode(output_step1[0], skip_special_tokens=True)
response_step2 = tokenizer.decode(output_step2[0], skip_special_tokens=True)
response_step3 = tokenizer.decode(output_step3[0], skip_special_tokens=True)

print(f"Step 1 Response: {response_step1}")
print(f"Step 2 Response: {response_step2}")
print(f"Step 3 Response: {response_step3}")
```

MAINTAINING MODEL PERFORMANCE OVER TIME

Challenge: AI models can experience performance degradation over time due to changes in data patterns and user interactions.

Strategies to Maintain Performance:

1. **Regular Updates:**
   - Continuously update models with new data to reflect current trends and patterns.
   - Perform periodic retraining to maintain model accuracy and relevance.
2. **Monitoring and Feedback:**
   - Implement monitoring systems to track model performance metrics.
   - Use user feedback to identify and address performance issues.
3. **Scalability:**
   - Design models and prompts that can scale effectively with increasing data and user interactions.
   - Optimize computational resources to handle larger workloads.

Example Implementation:

python

code

```python
def monitor_model_performance(model, prompts, expected_responses):
    performance_metrics = []
    for prompt, expected in zip(prompts, expected_responses):
        input_ids = tokenizer.encode(prompt, return_tensors='pt')
        output = model.generate(input_ids, max_length=50, num_return_sequences=1)
        response = tokenizer.decode(output[0], skip_special_tokens=True)

        # Simple performance metric example: string similarity
        similarity_score = compute_similarity(response, expected)
        performance_metrics.append(similarity_score)

    avg_performance = sum(performance_metrics) / len(performance_metrics)
    print(f"Average Performance Score: {avg_performance:.2f}")

prompts = ["What is photosynthesis?", "Explain the role of DNA in genetics.", "Describe the process of evaporation."]
expected_responses = ["Photosynthesis is the process by which plants...", "DNA is the molecule that carries genetic...", "Evaporation is the process where liquid water..."]

monitor_model_performance(model, prompts, expected_responses)
```

CONCLUSION

Addressing the challenges in prompt engineering is crucial for developing robust, reliable, and ethical AI systems. By employing strategies to overcome ambiguity, bias, complexity, and performance degradation, practitioners can enhance the effectiveness and trustworthiness of their models. This chapter provided practical insights and coding implementations to tackle these challenges, laying the groundwork for advanced prompt engineering practices.

In the following chapters, we will continue to explore additional topics, including domain-specific prompt engineering, collaborative AI systems, and the future of AI-driven interactions. Each chapter will build on the concepts introduced previously, offering new insights and practical applications to further enhance the effectiveness of AI models in diverse contexts.

CHAPTER 17: DOMAIN-SPECIFIC PROMPT ENGINEERING

INTRODUCTION TO DOMAIN- SPECIFIC PROMPT ENGINEERING

Domain-specific prompt engineering involves tailoring prompts to meet the unique requirements and challenges of specific fields or industries. By focusing on the particularities of a domain, practitioners can design prompts that enhance the relevance, accuracy, and effectiveness of AI models in specialized applications. This chapter will explore the principles and techniques for developing domain-specific prompts across various fields.

HEALTHCARE AND MEDICAL APPLICATIONS

Challenges in Healthcare Prompt Engineering:

- **Accuracy and Precision:** Medical information must be precise and reliable to ensure patient safety.
- **Ethical Considerations:** Protecting patient privacy and addressing biases in medical data are paramount.
- **Complexity:** Medical tasks often involve complex decision-making processes and detailed information.

Strategies for Healthcare Prompts:

1. **Incorporate Medical Terminology:**
   o Use precise medical terms and definitions to ensure clarity and accuracy.
   o Example Prompt: "Explain the pathophysiology of type 2 diabetes mellitus."
2. **Contextual Prompts:**
   o Provide detailed patient context to guide the AI's responses.
   o Example Prompt: "Given a patient with a history of hypertension and diabetes, outline the potential complications and recommended management strategies."
3. **Ethical Considerations:**
   o Ensure prompts are designed to protect patient

confidentiality and data security.

o   Example Prompt: "Describe the ethical considerations involved in sharing patient data for research purposes."

Implementation:

python
code

```
medical_prompt = "Explain the pathophysiology of type 2 diabetes mellitus."
input_ids = tokenizer.encode(medical_prompt, return_tensors='pt')
output = model.generate(input_ids, max_length=100, num_return_sequences=1)
response = tokenizer.decode(output[0], skip_special_tokens=True)
print(f"Medical Response: {response}")
```

FINANCIAL AND LEGAL DOMAINS

Challenges in Financial and Legal Prompt Engineering:

- **Regulatory Compliance:** Ensuring that AI-generated responses comply with legal and financial regulations.
- **Precision:** Financial and legal tasks require high levels of precision and detail.
- **Context Sensitivity:** Understanding the specific context of financial transactions or legal cases is crucial.

Strategies for Financial and Legal Prompts:

1. **Regulatory Context:**
   o   Include relevant regulations and compliance guidelines in prompts.
   o   Example Prompt: "Explain the key compliance requirements for GDPR in data processing."
2. **Detailed Instructions:**
   o   Provide detailed and specific instructions to guide the AI's responses.
   o   Example Prompt: "Outline the steps involved in the due diligence process for a merger and acquisition deal."
3. **Contextual Information:**
   o   Ensure that prompts include sufficient context about the financial or legal scenario.
   o   Example Prompt: "Given the following financial data, analyze the company's financial health and

suggest potential improvements."

Implementation:

python
  code

```
financial_prompt = "Outline the steps involved in the due diligence process for a merger and acquisition deal."
input_ids = tokenizer.encode(financial_prompt, return_tensors='pt')
output = model.generate(input_ids, max_length=100, num_return_sequences=1)
response = tokenizer.decode(output[0], skip_special_tokens=True)
print(f"Financial Response: {response}")
```

EDUCATIONAL APPLICATIONS

Challenges in Educational Prompt Engineering:

- **Adaptability:** Educational content must be adaptable to different learning levels and styles.
- **Engagement:** Prompts should be designed to engage and motivate learners.
- **Accuracy:** Ensuring the accuracy and reliability of educational content is critical.

Strategies for Educational Prompts:

1. **Tailored Content:**
   o Design prompts that adapt to different educational levels and learning styles.
   o Example Prompt: "Explain the concept of photosynthesis in simple terms for a fifth-grade student."
2. **Engaging and Interactive Prompts:**
   o Use prompts that encourage interaction and engagement with the content.
   o Example Prompt: "Create an interactive quiz on the basic principles of physics for high school students."
3. **Accurate and Reliable Information:**
   o Ensure that prompts guide the AI to generate accurate and up-to-date educational content.
   o Example Prompt: "Describe the latest advancements in renewable energy technologies."

Implementation:

python
   code

```
educational_prompt = "Explain the concept of photosynthesis
in simple terms for a fifth-grade student."
input_ids      =      tokenizer.encode(educational_prompt,
return_tensors='pt')
output    =    model.generate(input_ids,    max_length=100,
num_return_sequences=1)
response            =            tokenizer.decode(output[0],
skip_special_tokens=True)
print(f"Educational Response: {response}")
```

CREATIVE AND ARTISTIC DOMAINS

Challenges in Creative and Artistic Prompt Engineering:

- **Creativity and Innovation:** Prompts should encourage creativity and innovative thinking.
- **Subjectivity:** Creative tasks often involve subjective elements that are challenging to quantify.
- **Balance:** Balancing guidance with creative freedom is crucial.

Strategies for Creative and Artistic Prompts:

1. **Open-Ended Prompts:**
   o Use open-ended prompts to foster creativity and exploration.
   o Example Prompt: "Write a short story set in a dystopian future where technology controls every aspect of human life."
2. **Inspiration and References:**
   o Provide inspiration or references to guide creative outputs.
   o Example Prompt: "Compose a poem inspired by the themes of nature and solitude, similar to the works of William Wordsworth."
3. **Balancing Guidance and Freedom:**
   o Offer guidelines while allowing room for creative interpretation.
   o Example Prompt: "Design a poster for an upcoming

music festival, focusing on vibrant colors and a dynamic layout."

Implementation:

python
code

```
creative_prompt = "Write a short story set in a dystopian future where technology controls every aspect of human life."
input_ids = tokenizer.encode(creative_prompt, return_tensors='pt')
output = model.generate(input_ids, max_length=200, num_return_sequences=1)
response = tokenizer.decode(output[0], skip_special_tokens=True)
print(f"Creative Response: {response}")
```

CONCLUSION

Domain-specific prompt engineering requires a nuanced understanding of the unique challenges and requirements of different fields. By employing tailored strategies and techniques, practitioners can design prompts that enhance the effectiveness and relevance of AI models in specialized applications. This chapter provided a comprehensive overview of domain-specific prompt engineering, offering practical insights and coding examples to guide practitioners in various industries.

CHAPTER 18: COLLABORATIVE AI SYSTEMS AND PROMPT ENGINEERING

INTRODUCTION TO COLLABORATIVE AI SYSTEMS

Collaborative AI systems involve human-AI interactions where both parties work together to achieve common goals. These systems leverage the strengths of AI models and human expertise to enhance decision-making, problem-solving, and creativity. Prompt engineering plays a crucial role in designing effective collaborative AI systems. This chapter will explore strategies and techniques for developing prompts that facilitate seamless and productive collaboration between humans and AI.

HUMAN-AI COLLABORATION PRINCIPLES

Principles of Effective Human-AI Collaboration:

- **Complementarity:** AI and humans should complement each other's strengths. AI can handle data processing and pattern recognition, while humans provide context, judgment, and creativity.
- **Transparency:** AI systems should be transparent in their operations, making it easy for humans to understand and trust their outputs.
- **Interactivity:** Collaborative AI systems should support interactive and iterative processes, allowing humans to refine and guide AI outputs.

DESIGNING PROMPTS FOR HUMAN-AI COLLABORATION

Strategies for Designing Collaborative Prompts:

1. **Interactive Prompts:**
   o   Design prompts that encourage iterative interactions between humans and AI.
   o   Example Prompt: "Suggest three potential marketing strategies for our new product. I will review and provide feedback on each."

2. **Contextual Prompts:**
   o   Provide detailed context to guide AI outputs and align them with human goals.
   o   Example Prompt: "Based on the latest market research data, generate a report highlighting key trends and opportunities in the tech industry."

3. **Feedback Loops:**
   o   Incorporate mechanisms for humans to provide feedback and refine AI responses.
   o   Example Prompt: "Draft an initial project plan for our upcoming campaign. I will review and make adjustments as needed."

Implementation:

python
  code

```
collaborative_prompt = "Suggest three potential marketing
strategies for our new product. I will review and provide
feedback on each."
input_ids        =        tokenizer.encode(collaborative_prompt,
return_tensors='pt')
output   =   model.generate(input_ids,   max_length=150,
num_return_sequences=3)
responses = [tokenizer.decode(o, skip_special_tokens=True)
for o in output]

for i, response in enumerate(responses):
    print(f"Strategy {i+1}: {response}")
    # Simulate human feedback loop
    feedback = input(f"Provide feedback for Strategy {i+1}: ")
    # Integrate feedback into the next iteration (simplified for
demonstration)
    print(f"Refined Strategy {i+1} based on feedback: {response}
- Feedback: {feedback}")
```

ENHANCING TRUST AND TRANSPARENCY

Building Trust in Collaborative AI Systems:

- **Explainability:** Ensure that AI models can explain their outputs and decision-making processes.
- **Reliability:** Design prompts that produce consistent and reliable results.
- **Ethical Considerations:** Address ethical concerns, including bias and fairness, in prompt design and AI outputs.

Strategies for Enhancing Trust and Transparency:

1. **Explainable AI (XAI):**
   - Use techniques that make AI outputs more understandable and interpretable for humans.
   - Example Prompt: "Generate a summary of the financial report and explain the key factors influencing the company's performance."
2. **Consistency Checks:**
   - Implement consistency checks to ensure reliable AI outputs.
   - Example Prompt: "Provide a summary of the research findings. Ensure the key points are consistent with the data provided."
3. **Ethical Design:**
   - Design prompts that consider ethical implications and promote fairness.

o   Example Prompt: "Develop an inclusive hiring strategy that ensures diversity and equity in the recruitment process."

Implementation:

python
  code

```
trust_prompt = "Generate a summary of the financial report and explain the key factors influencing the company's performance."
input_ids = tokenizer.encode(trust_prompt, return_tensors='pt')
output = model.generate(input_ids, max_length=150, num_return_sequences=1)
response = tokenizer.decode(output[0], skip_special_tokens=True)
print(f"Explainable AI Response: {response}")
```

CASE STUDIES IN COLLABORATIVE AI SYSTEMS

Case Study 1: Collaborative Content Creation

Scenario: A marketing team collaborates with an AI tool to create content for a new campaign.

Objective: Design prompts that facilitate the iterative development of marketing materials.

Implementation:

1. **Initial Prompt:**
   o   "Draft an initial social media post to promote our new product. Focus on its key features and benefits."
2. **Human Feedback:**
   o   "The post is good, but can you emphasize the eco-friendly aspects more?"
3. **Refined Prompt:**
   o   "Revise the social media post to highlight the eco-friendly features of our new product more prominently."

Outcome: The AI tool and the marketing team collaboratively develop a compelling and targeted social media post.

Case Study 2: Collaborative Research Analysis

Scenario: A research team uses an AI assistant to analyze and summarize large datasets.

Objective: Design prompts that guide the AI to provide accurate and insightful analyses.

Implementation:

1. **Initial Prompt:**
   o "Analyze the provided dataset on climate change impacts and summarize the key findings."
2. **Human Feedback:**
   o "Include more details on regional variations in the impacts."
3. **Refined Prompt:**
   o "Update the summary to include detailed information on regional variations in climate change impacts."

Outcome: The AI assistant and the research team collaboratively produce a comprehensive and detailed analysis of the dataset.

CONCLUSION

Collaborative AI systems represent the future of human-AI interaction, where both parties work together to achieve superior outcomes. By designing prompts that facilitate effective collaboration, transparency, and trust, practitioners can harness the full potential of AI while leveraging human expertise. This chapter provided strategies, case studies, and coding implementations to guide the development of collaborative AI systems, enhancing their effectiveness and reliability.

CHAPTER 19: THE FUTURE OF AI-DRIVEN INTERACTIONS

INTRODUCTION
TO THE FUTURE
OF AI-DRIVEN
INTERACTIONS

As AI technology continues to evolve, the future of AI-driven interactions promises unprecedented advancements in various fields. This chapter will explore emerging trends, potential applications, and the future impact of AI-driven interactions. By understanding these developments, practitioners can stay ahead of the curve and leverage AI to its fullest potential.

EMERGING TRENDS IN AI-DRIVEN INTERACTIONS

Key Emerging Trends:

1. **Multimodal AI:**
   o   Integration of multiple data types, such as text, images, audio, and video, to enhance AI interactions.
   o   Example: AI systems that can analyze and generate multimedia content for richer user experiences.
2. **Context-Aware AI:**
   o   AI systems that understand and adapt to the context of interactions, providing more relevant and personalized responses.
   o   Example: Virtual assistants that consider user preferences, location, and past interactions to deliver tailored services.
3. **Emotionally Intelligent AI:**
   o   AI models that can recognize and respond to human emotions, improving user engagement and satisfaction.
   o   Example: Customer support bots that detect frustration or satisfaction in user tone and adjust their responses accordingly.

Implementation:

python

code

```
# Multimodal Prompt Example
multimodal_prompt = "Analyze this image and generate a
descriptive caption. Then, summarize the text in the attached
document."
# Assume functions to process image and text inputs
image_analysis = analyze_image('path/to/image.jpg')
text_summary = summarize_text('path/to/document.txt')

input_prompt = f"Image Analysis: {image_analysis}\nText
Summary: {text_summary}"
input_ids            =            tokenizer.encode(input_prompt,
return_tensors='pt')
output  =  model.generate(input_ids,  max_length=200,
num_return_sequences=1)
response            =            tokenizer.decode(output[0],
skip_special_tokens=True)
print(f"Multimodal AI Response: {response}")
```

POTENTIAL APPLICATIONS OF FUTURE AI INTERACTIONS

Healthcare and Wellbeing:

- **Personalized Health Assistants:**
  - AI-driven health assistants that provide personalized health advice, monitor patient conditions, and suggest preventive measures.
  - Example: AI systems that analyze patient data from wearable devices and provide real-time health recommendations.

Education and Learning:

- **Adaptive Learning Systems:**
  - AI-powered educational platforms that adapt to individual learning styles and progress, offering personalized learning experiences.
  - Example: Virtual tutors that provide customized lesson plans and real-time feedback to students.

Business and Commerce:

- **Intelligent Customer Engagement:**
  - AI systems that enhance customer engagement through personalized marketing,

predictive analytics, and proactive support.

o   Example: AI chatbots that predict customer needs and offer personalized product recommendations.

Implementation:

python
  code

```
# Personalized Health Assistant Prompt Example
health_prompt = "Analyze the patient's heart rate and activity data from the wearable device and provide personalized health advice."
input_ids = tokenizer.encode(health_prompt, return_tensors='pt')
output = model.generate(input_ids, max_length=150, num_return_sequences=1)
response = tokenizer.decode(output[0], skip_special_tokens=True)
print(f"Personalized Health Assistant Response: {response}")
```

FUTURE IMPACT OF AI-DRIVEN INTERACTIONS

Enhancing Human Capabilities:

- AI will augment human capabilities, enabling individuals to achieve more with less effort. From automating routine tasks to providing expert-level insights, AI-driven interactions will enhance productivity and innovation across various domains.

Ethical and Societal Considerations:

- As AI becomes more integrated into daily life, ethical considerations will become increasingly important. Ensuring fairness, transparency, and accountability in AI systems will be critical to gaining public trust and maximizing the positive impact of AI-driven interactions.

Continuous Learning and Adaptation:

- The future of AI-driven interactions will involve continuous learning and adaptation. AI systems will evolve in real-time, learning from user interactions and environmental changes to provide increasingly relevant and accurate responses.

Implementation:

python

code

```
# Continuous Learning and Adaptation Prompt Example
adaptation_prompt = "Based on recent user interactions and
feedback, suggest improvements to the AI system's response
generation."
input_ids = tokenizer.encode(adaptation_prompt,
return_tensors='pt')
output = model.generate(input_ids, max_length=150,
num_return_sequences=1)
response = tokenizer.decode(output[0],
skip_special_tokens=True)
print(f"Continuous Learning and Adaptation Response:
{response}")
```

CONCLUSION

The future of AI-driven interactions is poised to revolutionize various aspects of life and work. By understanding emerging trends, potential applications, and their impact, practitioners can prepare for and leverage these advancements to enhance AI systems' effectiveness and relevance. This chapter provided a forward-looking perspective on AI-driven interactions, offering insights and practical examples to guide the development of next-generation AI systems.

In the subsequent chapters, we will delve into specific use cases, advanced methodologies, and the integration of cutting-edge technologies in prompt engineering and AI interactions. Each chapter will build on the foundational knowledge and advanced strategies discussed previously, providing a comprehensive guide to mastering prompt engineering and AI-driven interactions in an ever-evolving landscape.

CHAPTER 20: INTEGRATING CUTTING-EDGE TECHNOLOGIES IN PROMPT ENGINEERING

INTRODUCTION TO INTEGRATION

As artificial intelligence continues to evolve, integrating cutting-edge technologies into prompt engineering is crucial for maximizing the capabilities and potential of AI models. This chapter explores the integration of advanced technologies such as quantum computing, federated learning, and edge AI into prompt engineering practices. By leveraging these technologies, practitioners can enhance the performance, efficiency, and applicability of AI systems in various domains.

QUANTUM COMPUTING AND PROMPT ENGINEERING

Overview of Quantum Computing:

Quantum computing leverages the principles of quantum mechanics to perform computations at unprecedented speeds. Unlike classical computing, which uses bits as the smallest unit of information, quantum computing uses qubits that can represent multiple states simultaneously, enabling parallel computations.

Applications in Prompt Engineering:

1. **Optimization:**
   o   Quantum computing can optimize prompt generation and model training processes by solving complex optimization problems more efficiently than classical computers.
   o   Example: Using quantum algorithms to optimize hyperparameters for prompt-based models, resulting in faster and more accurate training.
2. **Enhanced Data Processing:**
   o   Quantum computing can process large datasets more quickly, enabling real-time prompt engineering for dynamic applications.

○   Example: Real-time analysis and prompt generation for high-frequency trading in financial markets.

Implementation:

python
   code

```
# Example of integrating quantum computing for prompt optimization
from qiskit import Aer, transpile, assemble
from qiskit.algorithms import VQE
from qiskit.circuit.library import RealAmplitudes
from qiskit.optimization import QuadraticProgram

# Define an optimization problem
problem = QuadraticProgram()
# Add variables and constraints to the problem
# ...

# Use a quantum algorithm to solve the optimization problem
backend = Aer.get_backend('qasm_simulator')
quantum_algorithm        =        VQE(RealAmplitudes(),
optimizer='COBYLA', quantum_instance=backend)
result = quantum_algorithm.solve(problem)

print(f"Optimized Solution: {result}")
```

FEDERATED LEARNING IN PROMPT ENGINEERING

Overview of Federated Learning:

Federated learning is a decentralized approach to machine learning where multiple devices collaboratively train a model without sharing their data. This technique enhances privacy and security by keeping data localized while leveraging the collective knowledge of distributed datasets.

Applications in Prompt Engineering:

1. **Privacy-Preserving Prompts:**
   - Federated learning allows the development of prompt-based models that respect user privacy by training on decentralized data without central aggregation.
   - Example: Developing healthcare prompts that learn from patient data across multiple hospitals without compromising patient privacy.
2. **Collaborative Training:**
   - Federated learning enables collaborative training of prompt-based models across different organizations or user groups, enhancing model robustness and generalizability.

o   Example: Training a multilingual prompt-based translation model using data from diverse linguistic communities.

Implementation:

python
  code

```
# Example of federated learning for training prompt-based
models
from federated_learning import FederatedModel

# Define the model and data sources
model = FederatedModel(model_architecture='transformer')
data_sources    =    ['hospital_1_data',    'hospital_2_data',
'hospital_3_data']

# Train the model using federated learning
model.train(data_sources, epochs=10)

print("Federated Model Training Complete")
```

EDGE AI AND PROMPT ENGINEERING

Overview of Edge AI:

Edge AI involves deploying AI models on edge devices, such as smartphones, IoT devices, and edge servers, to perform computations locally. This approach reduces latency, enhances privacy, and enables real-time decision-making by processing data close to its source.

Applications in Prompt Engineering:

1. **Real-Time Prompts:**
   - Edge AI enables the deployment of prompt-based models on edge devices for real-time applications, such as autonomous vehicles, smart cities, and industrial automation.
   - Example: Using edge AI to generate real-time prompts for navigation and safety in autonomous vehicles.

2. **Reduced Latency:**
   - By processing prompts locally, edge AI reduces latency and improves the responsiveness of AI systems in critical applications.
   - Example: Generating immediate prompts for emergency response systems in smart cities.

Implementation:

python
   code
```
# Example of deploying prompt-based models on edge devices
from edge_ai import EdgeModel

# Define the model and edge device
model    =    EdgeModel(model_architecture='transformer',
device='raspberry_pi')

# Deploy the model to the edge device
model.deploy()

# Generate prompts in real-time on the edge device
prompt = "Analyze the sensor data and provide safety
recommendations."
response = model.generate(prompt)
print(f"Edge AI Response: {response}")
```

INTEGRATING BLOCKCHAIN FOR SECURE PROMPT ENGINEERING

Overview of Blockchain:

Blockchain is a decentralized and immutable ledger technology that ensures transparency, security, and traceability of transactions. Integrating blockchain with prompt engineering can enhance the security and reliability of AI interactions.

Applications in Prompt Engineering:

1. **Secure Data Sharing:**
   o   Blockchain enables secure and transparent sharing of data used for prompt engineering, ensuring data integrity and provenance.
   o   Example: Using blockchain to securely share medical data for training healthcare prompts.
2. **Auditability:**
   o   Blockchain provides a transparent and auditable record of prompt generation and model training processes, enhancing trust and accountability.
   o   Example: Maintaining an auditable log of changes and updates to prompt-based models in legal and financial applications.

Implementation:

python
　code

```python
# Example of integrating blockchain for secure prompt
engineering
from blockchain import Blockchain

# Initialize blockchain for secure data sharing
blockchain = Blockchain()

# Add data to the blockchain
data_entry = {"prompt": "Generate a report on climate change
impacts.", "timestamp": "2024-07-17"}
blockchain.add_data(data_entry)

# Verify and audit data entries
audit_log = blockchain.get_audit_log()
print(f"Blockchain Audit Log: {audit_log}")
```

CONCLUSION

Integrating cutting-edge technologies such as quantum computing, federated learning, edge AI, and blockchain into prompt engineering practices can significantly enhance the capabilities, security, and efficiency of AI models. This chapter provided a comprehensive overview of these technologies and their applications in prompt engineering, along with practical coding examples to guide practitioners in leveraging these advancements. By staying at the forefront of technological innovation, practitioners can push the boundaries of what is possible with AI-driven interactions.

CHAPTER 21: ADVANCED METHODOLOGIES IN PROMPT ENGINEERING

INTRODUCTION TO ADVANCED METHODOLOGIES

Advanced methodologies in prompt engineering involve sophisticated techniques and approaches that push the boundaries of AI capabilities. This chapter will delve into advanced methodologies such as reinforcement learning, generative adversarial networks (GANs), and meta-learning. By mastering these methodologies, practitioners can enhance the effectiveness, adaptability, and innovation of prompt-based AI systems.

REINFORCEMENT LEARNING IN PROMPT ENGINEERING

Overview of Reinforcement Learning (RL):

Reinforcement learning is a type of machine learning where an agent learns to make decisions by taking actions in an environment to maximize cumulative rewards. RL is particularly useful for tasks that require sequential decision-making and optimization over time.

Applications in Prompt Engineering:

1. **Optimizing Prompt Strategies:**
   o   RL can optimize the sequence and structure of prompts to achieve desired outcomes, such as maximizing user engagement or accuracy in responses.
   o   Example: Using RL to develop a strategy for adaptive learning systems that personalize prompts based on student performance.
2. **Interactive Dialogues:**
   o   RL can enhance interactive dialogue systems by learning from user interactions and feedback to improve the relevance and coherence of responses.
   o   Example: Training a customer support chatbot

to dynamically adjust its prompts based on user satisfaction and engagement metrics.

Implementation:

python
  code

```python
# Example of using reinforcement learning for prompt optimization
import gym
from stable_baselines3 import PPO

# Define a custom RL environment for prompt engineering
class PromptEnv(gym.Env):
    def __init__(self):
        super(PromptEnv, self).__init__()
        self.action_space = gym.spaces.Discrete(10)
        self.observation_space = gym.spaces.Box(low=0, high=1, shape=(10,), dtype=np.float32)

    def step(self, action):
        # Implement the environment's step logic
        reward = self.calculate_reward(action)
        done = self.check_done()
        return self.state, reward, done, {}

    def reset(self):
        # Reset the environment state
        self.state = self.get_initial_state()
        return self.state

    def calculate_reward(self, action):
        # Calculate the reward based on the action taken
        return reward

    def check_done(self):
        # Check if the episode is done
        return done

# Train the RL model
env = PromptEnv()
```

```
model = PPO('MlpPolicy', env, verbose=1)
model.learn(total_timesteps=10000)

# Use the trained model to generate optimized prompts
optimized_prompt = model.predict(env.reset())
print(f"Optimized Prompt: {optimized_prompt}")
```

GENERATIVE ADVERSARIAL NETWORKS (GANS) IN PROMPT ENGINEERING

Overview of GANs:

Generative adversarial networks (GANs) consist of two neural networks, a generator and a discriminator, that compete against each other to create realistic data. GANs are powerful tools for generating high-quality synthetic data and enhancing creative applications.

Applications in Prompt Engineering:

1. **Synthetic Data Generation:**
   o   GANs can generate synthetic data to augment training datasets, improving the robustness and diversity of prompt-based models.
   o   Example: Using GANs to generate diverse and representative training prompts for multilingual language models.
2. **Creative Content Generation:**
   o   GANs can enhance creative applications by generating novel and high-quality content based on

specified prompts.

o   Example: Using GANs to create artistic images or music compositions based on textual prompts.

Implementation:

python
  code

```
# Example of using GANs for synthetic data generation
import torch
import torch.nn as nn
import torch.optim as optim

# Define the generator and discriminator networks
class Generator(nn.Module):
    def __init__(self):
        super(Generator, self).__init__()
        self.main = nn.Sequential(
            nn.Linear(100, 256),
            nn.ReLU(True),
            nn.Linear(256, 512),
            nn.ReLU(True),
            nn.Linear(512, 784),
            nn.Tanh()
        )

    def forward(self, input):
        return self.main(input)

class Discriminator(nn.Module):
    def __init__(self):
        super(Discriminator, self).__init__()
        self.main = nn.Sequential(
            nn.Linear(784, 512),
            nn.LeakyReLU(0.2, inplace=True),
            nn.Linear(512, 256),
            nn.LeakyReLU(0.2, inplace=True),
            nn.Linear(256, 1),
            nn.Sigmoid()
        )
```

```python
    def forward(self, input):
        return self.main(input)

# Initialize the networks and optimizers
netG = Generator()
netD = Discriminator()
optimizerG = optim.Adam(netG.parameters(), lr=0.0002)
optimizerD = optim.Adam(netD.parameters(), lr=0.0002)
criterion = nn.BCELoss()

# Train the GAN
for epoch in range(10000):
    # Train the discriminator
    optimizerD.zero_grad()
    real_data = torch.randn(64, 784)
    fake_data = netG(torch.randn(64, 100))
    real_label = torch.ones(64, 1)
    fake_label = torch.zeros(64, 1)
    real_output = netD(real_data)
    fake_output = netD(fake_data)
    lossD_real = criterion(real_output, real_label)
    lossD_fake = criterion(fake_output, fake_label)
    lossD = lossD_real + lossD_fake
    lossD.backward()
    optimizerD.step()

    # Train the generator
    optimizerG.zero_grad()
    fake_data = netG(torch.randn(64, 100))
    fake_output = netD(fake_data)
    lossG = criterion(fake_output, real_label)
    lossG.backward()
    optimizerG.step()

print("GAN Training Complete")
```

META-LEARNING IN PROMPT ENGINEERING

Overview of Meta-Learning:

Meta-learning, or "learning to learn," involves training models to quickly adapt to new tasks with minimal data. Meta-learning is particularly useful for prompt engineering, as it enables models to generalize across diverse tasks and domains.

Applications in Prompt Engineering:

1. **Few-Shot Prompt Adaptation:**
   o   Meta-learning allows models to adapt prompts for new tasks with minimal examples, enhancing flexibility and efficiency.
   o   Example: Training a meta-learning model to generate effective prompts for novel applications, such as emerging research topics.
2. **Cross-Domain Generalization:**
   o   Meta-learning enables models to generalize prompts across different domains, improving versatility and applicability.
   o   Example: Using meta-learning to develop prompts that work across various industries, from healthcare to finance.

Implementation:

python
code

```python
# Example of using meta-learning for prompt adaptation
import learn2learn as l2l

# Define a meta-learning model using MAML (Model-Agnostic
Meta-Learning)
class PromptModel(nn.Module):
    def __init__(self):
        super(PromptModel, self).__init__()
        self.fc1 = nn.Linear(10, 20)
        self.fc2 = nn.Linear(20, 1)

    def forward(self, x):
        x = torch.relu(self.fc1(x))
        x = self.fc2(x)
        return x

model = PromptModel()
maml = l2l.algorithms.MAML(model, lr=0.01)

# Meta-training loop
for task in range(100):
    learner = maml.clone()
    for step in range(10):
        # Sample a task and compute the loss
        task_data = sample_task_data()
        loss = compute_loss(learner(task_data))
        learner.adapt(loss)

    # Update the meta-model
    meta_loss = compute_meta_loss(learner, meta_task_data)
    meta_loss.backward()
    maml.step()

print("Meta-Learning Training Complete")
```

CONCLUSION

Advanced methodologies such as reinforcement learning, generative adversarial networks, and meta-learning offer powerful tools for enhancing prompt engineering. By mastering these techniques, practitioners can develop more effective, adaptable, and innovative prompt-based AI systems. This chapter provided a comprehensive overview of these methodologies, along with practical coding examples, to guide practitioners in leveraging advanced approaches in prompt engineering.

CHAPTER 22:
BUILDING ROBUST
AND RELIABLE
PROMPT-BASED
MODELS

INTRODUCTION TO ROBUSTNESS AND RELIABILITY

Robustness and reliability are critical attributes for prompt-based AI models, ensuring consistent performance across diverse scenarios and minimizing the risk of failures or inaccuracies. This chapter explores strategies and techniques for building robust and reliable prompt-based models, including error handling, validation methods, and continuous improvement practices.

ERROR HANDLING AND RECOVERY

Strategies for Effective Error Handling:

1. Predefined Error Responses:
o   Design prompts that include predefined responses for common errors or uncertainties, ensuring that the model can handle unexpected inputs gracefully.
o   Example: "I'm sorry, I didn't understand that. Could you please rephrase your question?"

2. Context-Aware Error Detection:
o   Implement context-aware error detection mechanisms to identify and correct errors in real-time.
o   Example: Detecting and correcting grammatical errors or factual inaccuracies in the model's responses.

Implementation:

python
  code
```
# Example of implementing error handling in prompt-based
models
def generate_response_with_error_handling(prompt):
    try:
        input_ids         =              tokenizer.encode(prompt,
return_tensors='pt')
        output  =  model.generate(input_ids,  max_length=50,
num_return_sequences=1)
```

```
        response        =        tokenizer.decode(output[0],
skip_special_tokens=True)
        # Implement context-aware error detection
        if detect_errors(response):
            raise ValueError("Detected error in response")
        return response
    except Exception as e:
        return f"Error: {str(e)}. Please try rephrasing your
question."

prompt = "Explain the impact of climate change on polar
bears."
response = generate_response_with_error_handling(prompt)
print(f"Response: {response}")
```

VALIDATION METHODS FOR PROMPT-BASED MODELS

Techniques for Validating Model Outputs:

1. **Automated Validation:**
   o   Use automated validation techniques such as unit tests, integration tests, and end-to-end tests to ensure the correctness and reliability of model outputs.
   o   Example: Implementing test cases that verify the accuracy and relevance of responses to specific prompts.

2. **Human-in-the-Loop Validation:**
   o   Incorporate human evaluators in the validation process to provide qualitative feedback and identify issues that automated methods might miss.
   o   Example: Conducting user studies to assess the clarity, accuracy, and usefulness of model responses.

Implementation:

```python
code
# Example of implementing automated validation for prompt-based models
```

```python
def validate_model_responses(prompts, expected_responses):
    for prompt, expected in zip(prompts, expected_responses):
        response = generate_response_with_error_handling(prompt)
        assert response == expected, f"Validation failed for prompt: {prompt}"

prompts = ["What is the capital of France?", "Who wrote 'To Kill a Mockingbird'?"]
expected_responses = ["The capital of France is Paris.", "'To Kill a Mockingbird' was written by Harper Lee."]

validate_model_responses(prompts, expected_responses)
print("Model validation complete")
```

CONTINUOUS IMPROVEMENT PRACTICES

Approaches to Continuous Improvement:

1. **Feedback Loops:**
   o   Implement continuous feedback loops to gather insights from users and iteratively improve prompts and model performance.
   o   Example: Collecting user feedback on the relevance and clarity of responses and using it to refine prompt designs.
2. **Performance Monitoring:**
   o   Regularly monitor model performance metrics to identify trends, detect anomalies, and address performance degradation.
   o   Example: Tracking metrics such as accuracy, response time, and user satisfaction over time.

Implementation:

python
  code
```
# Example of implementing continuous improvement
practices for prompt-based models
def collect_user_feedback(prompt, response):
    # Simulate collecting user feedback
    feedback = input(f"Feedback on response to prompt
```

```
'{prompt}': {response}\n")
    return feedback

def refine_prompt_based_on_feedback(prompt, feedback):
    # Simulate refining the prompt based on feedback
    refined_prompt = f"{prompt} (Adjusted based on feedback:
{feedback})"
    return refined_prompt

prompt = "Explain the significance of the Industrial
Revolution."
response = generate_response_with_error_handling(prompt)
feedback = collect_user_feedback(prompt, response)
refined_prompt = refine_prompt_based_on_feedback(prompt,
feedback)
print(f"Refined Prompt: {refined_prompt}")
```

ENSURING ETHICAL AND FAIR AI

Strategies for Ethical and Fair AI:

1. **Bias Mitigation:**
   o Implement strategies to identify and mitigate biases in prompts and model outputs, ensuring fairness and inclusivity.
   o Example: Using fairness metrics to evaluate model performance across different demographic groups.
2. **Transparency and Accountability:**
   o Ensure transparency in AI operations by providing explanations for model decisions and maintaining accountability for AI-driven outcomes.
   o Example: Implementing explainable AI techniques to make model outputs understandable and justifiable.

Implementation:

python
   code
```
# Example of implementing bias mitigation in prompt-based models
def evaluate_fairness(prompts, demographic_data):
    fairness_scores = []
    for prompt in prompts:
        response                                                    =
generate_response_with_error_handling(prompt)
        fairness_score    =    compute_fairness_score(response,
```

```
demographic_data)
    fairness_scores.append(fairness_score)
  avg_fairness_score      =      sum(fairness_scores)      /
len(fairness_scores)
  return avg_fairness_score

prompts = ["Describe a typical leader.", "Explain the
importance of diversity in the workplace."]
demographic_data = {"gender": ["male", "female"], "ethnicity":
["white", "non-white"]}

fairness_score             =             evaluate_fairness(prompts,
demographic_data)
print(f"Average Fairness Score: {fairness_score}")
```

CONCLUSION

Building robust and reliable prompt-based models is essential for ensuring consistent performance and minimizing the risk of failures or inaccuracies. By employing effective error handling, validation methods, continuous improvement practices, and ethical considerations, practitioners can develop AI systems that are both dependable and fair. This chapter provided strategies, techniques, and practical examples to guide the development of robust and reliable prompt-based models, enhancing their overall quality and trustworthiness.

CHAPTER 23: SCALING PROMPT ENGINEERING FOR LARGE-SCALE APPLICATIONS

INTRODUCTION TO SCALING

Scaling prompt engineering for large-scale applications involves designing and deploying AI models that can handle vast amounts of data, high user traffic, and complex tasks across diverse environments. This chapter explores strategies and techniques for scaling prompt engineering, including distributed computing, cloud-based deployment, and performance optimization. By mastering these approaches, practitioners can ensure their AI systems are efficient, scalable, and resilient.

DISTRIBUTED COMPUTING FOR PROMPT ENGINEERING

Overview of Distributed Computing:

Distributed computing involves using multiple interconnected computers to perform tasks concurrently, enhancing computational power and efficiency. This approach is essential for scaling AI models to handle large datasets and high workloads.

Applications in Prompt Engineering:

1. **Parallel Processing:**
   o   Distribute the processing of prompts and model training across multiple machines to improve speed and efficiency.
   o   Example: Using distributed computing frameworks such as Apache Spark or Dask to parallelize data preprocessing and prompt generation tasks.
2. **Scalability:**
   o   Scale AI models horizontally by adding more nodes to the computing cluster, ensuring the system can handle increased data and user demands.
   o   Example: Deploying a cluster of GPU-accelerated nodes to train large language models

more efficiently.

Implementation:

python
code

```python
# Example of using distributed computing for prompt
engineering with Dask
import dask.dataframe as dd

# Load and preprocess data using Dask
data = dd.read_csv('large_dataset.csv')
processed_data = data.map_partitions(preprocess_function)

# Generate prompts in parallel
def generate_prompt(row):
    prompt = f"Analyze the following data: {row['data']}"
    response = model.generate(prompt)
    return response

prompts = processed_data.map_partitions(generate_prompt)
print(prompts.compute())
```

CLOUD-BASED DEPLOYMENT FOR SCALABILITY

Overview of Cloud-Based Deployment:

Cloud-based deployment involves using cloud services to host and manage AI models, providing scalability, flexibility, and cost-efficiency. Cloud platforms such as AWS, Google Cloud, and Azure offer various tools and services to facilitate large-scale AI deployments.

Applications in Prompt Engineering:

1. **Elastic Scaling:**
   o   Utilize cloud services to automatically scale resources up or down based on demand, ensuring efficient use of computational resources.
   o   Example: Using AWS Auto Scaling to dynamically adjust the number of instances running a prompt-based model during peak and off-peak hours.
2. **High Availability:**
   o   Deploy AI models across multiple geographic regions to ensure high availability and fault tolerance.
   o   Example: Using Google Cloud's global load balancing to distribute user requests across multiple instances of a prompt-based model deployed in different regions.

Implementation:

python
  code

```
# Example of deploying a prompt-based model on AWS using
Boto3
import boto3

# Initialize the AWS client
ec2 = boto3.client('ec2')

# Launch an EC2 instance for the prompt-based model
instance = ec2.run_instances(
    ImageId='ami-0abcdef1234567890',
    InstanceType='t2.medium',
    MinCount=1,
    MaxCount=1,
    KeyName='my-key-pair'
)

# Deploy the model to the instance
instance_id = instance['Instances'][0]['InstanceId']
print(f"Deployed model on instance: {instance_id}")
```

PERFORMANCE OPTIMIZATION FOR LARGE-SCALE APPLICATIONS

Strategies for Performance Optimization:

1. Model Compression:
o   Use techniques such as quantization, pruning, and knowledge distillation to reduce the size and computational requirements of AI models without sacrificing performance.

o   Example: Applying quantization to a large language model to enable efficient inference on edge devices.

2. Caching and Preprocessing:
o   Implement caching mechanisms and preprocess data to reduce latency and improve response times.

o   Example: Caching frequently used prompts and responses to minimize redundant computations.

Implementation:

python
  code

```
# Example of implementing model compression using PyTorch
import torch
from torch.quantization import quantize_dynamic
```

```
# Load a pre-trained model
model = torch.load('large_language_model.pth')

# Apply dynamic quantization to the model
quantized_model          =          quantize_dynamic(model,
{torch.nn.Linear}, dtype=torch.qint8)

# Save the quantized model
torch.save(quantized_model,
'quantized_language_model.pth')
print("Model quantization complete")
```

MANAGING LARGE-SCALE DATA PIPELINES

Approaches to Managing Data Pipelines:

1. **Data Ingestion and ETL:**
   - Implement efficient data ingestion and ETL (extract, transform, load) processes to handle large volumes of data.
   - Example: Using Apache Kafka for real-time data ingestion and Apache Beam for ETL processing in a prompt-based recommendation system.
2. **Data Storage and Retrieval:**
   - Use scalable and efficient data storage solutions, such as distributed databases and data lakes, to manage and retrieve data.
   - Example: Storing prompt-related data in Amazon S3 and using Amazon Athena for fast and cost-effective querying.

Implementation:

python
code

```
# Example of managing data pipelines using Apache Kafka and
Apache Beam
from kafka import KafkaConsumer
import apache_beam as beam
```

```python
# Set up Kafka consumer for real-time data ingestion
consumer = KafkaConsumer('prompt_data', bootstrap_servers=['localhost:9092'])

# Define a Beam pipeline for ETL processing
def run_pipeline():
    with beam.Pipeline() as pipeline:
        (
            pipeline
            | 'Read from Kafka' >> beam.io.ReadFromKafka(consumer)
            | 'Extract data' >> beam.Map(lambda record: extract_data(record))
            | 'Transform data' >> beam.Map(lambda data: transform_data(data))
            | 'Load data' >> beam.io.WriteToText('output_data.txt')
        )

run_pipeline()
print("Data pipeline processing complete")
```

CONCLUSION

Scaling prompt engineering for large-scale applications requires a combination of distributed computing, cloud-based deployment, performance optimization, and efficient data pipeline management. By mastering these strategies and techniques, practitioners can ensure their AI systems are scalable, efficient, and resilient, capable of handling vast amounts of data and high user traffic. This chapter provided comprehensive insights and practical examples to guide the development and deployment of large-scale prompt-based models, enhancing their overall performance and scalability.

CHAPTER 24:
SECURITY AND
PRIVACY IN PROMPT
ENGINEERING

INTRODUCTION TO SECURITY AND PRIVACY

Ensuring security and privacy in prompt engineering is crucial to protect sensitive data, maintain user trust, and comply with regulatory requirements. This chapter explores best practices and techniques for securing prompt-based AI systems, including data encryption, access control, and privacy-preserving methods. By implementing robust security and privacy measures, practitioners can safeguard their AI models and user data from potential threats.

DATA ENCRYPTION AND SECURE COMMUNICATION

Techniques for Data Encryption:

1. **End-to-End Encryption:**
   - Implement end-to-end encryption to protect data during transmission, ensuring that only authorized parties can access the information.
   - Example: Using TLS (Transport Layer Security) to encrypt communication between clients and servers in a prompt-based AI system.
2. **Data Encryption at Rest:**
   - Encrypt data stored on disk to protect it from unauthorized access and breaches.
   - Example: Encrypting prompt-related data stored in databases using AES (Advanced Encryption Standard).

Implementation:

python
  code

```
# Example of implementing TLS for secure communication in a Flask web application
from flask import Flask, request
import ssl

app = Flask(__name__)
```

```python
@app.route('/generate_prompt', methods=['POST'])
def generate_prompt():
    prompt = request.json['prompt']
    response = model.generate(prompt)
    return response

if __name__ == '__main__':
    context = ssl.SSLContext(ssl.PROTOCOL_TLS)
    context.load_cert_chain('path/to/cert.pem',        'path/to/
key.pem')
    app.run(ssl_context=context)
print("Secure Flask application running with TLS")
```

ACCESS CONTROL AND AUTHENTICATION

Strategies for Access Control and Authentication:

1. **Role-Based Access Control (RBAC):**
   o   Implement RBAC to manage permissions based on user roles, ensuring that only authorized users can access specific functions and data.
   o   Example: Assigning different roles (e.g., admin, user, guest) with distinct permissions in a prompt-based AI system.
2. **Multi-Factor Authentication (MFA):**
   o   Use MFA to enhance security by requiring multiple forms of verification for user authentication.
   o   Example: Implementing MFA using passwords and one-time codes sent to users' mobile devices.

Implementation:

python
   code

```
# Example of implementing RBAC in a Django web application
from django.contrib.auth.models import User, Group
from django.shortcuts import render
from        django.contrib.auth.decorators        import
permission_required

def create_group(name, permissions):
```

```
    group, created = Group.objects.get_or_create(name=name)
    for permission in permissions:
        group.permissions.add(permission)
    return group

# Define permissions and create groups
admin_permissions = ['add_user', 'change_user', 'delete_user']
user_permissions = ['view_user']
create_group('admin', admin_permissions)
create_group('user', user_permissions)

@permission_required('view_user', raise_exception=True)
def generate_prompt(request):
    prompt = request.POST['prompt']
    response = model.generate(prompt)
    return    render(request,    'response.html',    {'response':
response})

print("RBAC implemented in Django application")
```

PRIVACY-PRESERVING METHODS

Approaches to Privacy Preservation:

1. **Differential Privacy:**
   - Implement differential privacy techniques to add noise to data, protecting individual privacy while preserving the utility of aggregated data.
   - Example: Applying differential privacy to anonymize user data used for training prompt-based models.

2. **Federated Learning:**
   - Use federated learning to train models on decentralized data, ensuring that raw data remains on local devices and only aggregated insights are shared.
   - Example: Developing prompt-based models for personalized recommendations without centralizing user data.

Implementation:

python
   code
```python
# Example of implementing differential privacy using PySyft
import torch
import syft as sy
```

```
# Initialize PySyft and create a virtual worker
hook = sy.TorchHook(torch)
worker = sy.VirtualWorker(hook, id='worker')

# Create a private dataset with differential privacy
data = torch.randn(100, 10)
private_data = data.fix_prec().share(worker)

# Train a model with differential privacy
model = syft.nn.Linear(10, 1)
optimizer = sy.optim.SGD(model.parameters(), lr=0.01)
for epoch in range(10):
    optimizer.zero_grad()
    output = model(private_data)
    loss = ((output - private_data) ** 2).sum()
    loss.backward()
    optimizer.step()

print("Model training with differential privacy complete")
```

COMPLIANCE WITH REGULATORY REQUIREMENTS

Ensuring Compliance with Regulations:

1. **GDPR Compliance:**
o   Implement measures to comply with the General Data Protection Regulation (GDPR), including data minimization, user consent, and the right to be forgotten.
o   Example: Ensuring prompt-based models allow users to request data deletion and manage their consent preferences.

2. **HIPAA Compliance:**
o   Implement measures to comply with the Health Insurance Portability and Accountability Act (HIPAA), ensuring the confidentiality, integrity, and availability of protected health information (PHI).
o   Example: Using encryption and access controls to protect PHI used in healthcare prompt-based models.

Implementation:

python
   code
```python
# Example of implementing GDPR compliance in a Flask web application
from flask import Flask, request, jsonify
```

```
app = Flask(__name__)

@app.route('/consent', methods=['POST'])
def manage_consent():
    user_id = request.json['user_id']
    consent = request.json['consent']
    # Store user consent preferences in the database
    store_consent(user_id, consent)
    return jsonify({'status': 'Consent preferences updated'})

@app.route('/delete_data', methods=['POST'])
def delete_data():
    user_id = request.json['user_id']
    # Delete user data from the database
    delete_user_data(user_id)
    return jsonify({'status': 'User data deleted'})

print("GDPR compliance implemented in Flask application")
```

CONCLUSION

Ensuring security and privacy in prompt engineering is essential for protecting sensitive data, maintaining user trust, and complying with regulatory requirements. By implementing robust data encryption, access control, privacy-preserving methods, and regulatory compliance measures, practitioners can safeguard their AI models and user data from potential threats. This chapter provided best practices, strategies, and practical examples to guide the development of secure and privacy-preserving prompt-based AI systems.

CHAPTER 25: THE ROAD AHEAD FOR PROMPT ENGINEERING

INTRODUCTION TO FUTURE DIRECTIONS

As we conclude this comprehensive guide on prompt engineering, it's essential to look ahead and explore the future directions and potential advancements in this field. This chapter will discuss emerging trends, ongoing research, and the future impact of prompt engineering on AI and society. By understanding these developments, practitioners can stay ahead of the curve and continue to innovate in prompt engineering.

EMERGING TRENDS IN PROMPT ENGINEERING

Key Emerging Trends:

1. **Adaptive and Context-Aware Prompts:**
   o   The development of AI models that adapt prompts in real-time based on user context and interactions, enhancing personalization and relevance.
   o   Example: AI systems that dynamically adjust prompts based on user behavior, preferences, and environmental factors.
2. **Interactive and Multimodal Prompts:**
   o   The integration of multimodal data (text, images, audio, etc.) in prompt engineering, enabling richer and more interactive AI interactions.
   o   Example: AI assistants that use voice and visual inputs to generate contextually appropriate prompts and responses.
3. **Ethical AI and Responsible Prompt Engineering:**
   o   The focus on ethical considerations and responsible AI practices in prompt engineering, ensuring fairness, transparency, and accountability.
   o   Example: Developing frameworks and guidelines for ethical prompt engineering that address bias, inclusivity, and user rights.

ONGOING RESEARCH IN PROMPT ENGINEERING

Areas of Ongoing Research:

1. **Advanced Natural Language Understanding:**
   o   Research on improving natural language understanding capabilities of AI models to handle more complex and nuanced prompts.
   o   Example: Developing models that can comprehend and generate responses to ambiguous, sarcastic, or context-dependent prompts.

2. **Zero-Shot and Few-Shot Learning:**
   o   Advances in zero-shot and few-shot learning techniques, enabling AI models to generate relevant responses to new and unseen prompts with minimal training data.
   o   Example: Training prompt-based models that can quickly adapt to new languages, domains, or tasks with limited data.

3. **Human-AI Collaboration:**
   o   Research on enhancing human-AI collaboration through improved prompt engineering, enabling more effective and seamless interactions between humans and AI.
   o   Example: Studying how different prompt designs impact user satisfaction, engagement, and

productivity in collaborative tasks.

FUTURE IMPACT OF PROMPT ENGINEERING

Potential Impact on Various Domains:

1. **Healthcare:**
   - The future of prompt engineering in healthcare promises more accurate, personalized, and proactive health management solutions.
   - Example: AI systems that generate prompts to guide patients through personalized treatment plans and lifestyle adjustments.

2. **Education:**
   - The integration of prompt engineering in education will enable more adaptive and engaging learning experiences, catering to diverse student needs.
   - Example: AI tutors that generate prompts to provide instant feedback, additional resources, and personalized learning paths.

3. **Business and Industry:**
   - Prompt engineering will drive innovation in business and industry by automating complex tasks, enhancing decision-making, and improving customer engagement.
   - Example: AI-driven business intelligence tools that generate prompts to identify market trends, optimize operations, and forecast demand.

PREPARING FOR THE FUTURE

Steps to Stay Ahead:

1. **Continuous Learning:**
   o   Stay updated with the latest research, trends, and advancements in prompt engineering and related fields.
   o   Example: Participating in conferences, workshops, and online courses on AI and prompt engineering.
2. **Innovation and Experimentation:**
   o   Foster a culture of innovation and experimentation within your organization or practice, encouraging the exploration of new ideas and approaches.
   o   Example: Setting up dedicated innovation labs to experiment with cutting-edge prompt engineering techniques and applications.
3. **Ethical Considerations:**
   o   Prioritize ethical considerations in all prompt engineering endeavors, ensuring that AI systems are fair, transparent, and accountable.
   o   Example: Developing and adhering to ethical guidelines and standards for prompt engineering practices.

CONCLUSION

The road ahead for prompt engineering is filled with exciting opportunities and challenges. By embracing emerging trends, ongoing research, and ethical considerations, practitioners can continue to innovate and push the boundaries of what is possible with AI-driven interactions. This chapter provided a forward-looking perspective on the future of prompt engineering, offering insights and recommendations to guide practitioners in their ongoing journey of mastery and innovation.

By following the comprehensive guidance provided in this book, developers, researchers, and NLP enthusiasts can master the art and science of prompt engineering, creating effective, ethical, and innovative AI systems that drive positive impact across various domains.

CHAPTER 26: ADVANCED CUSTOMIZATION TECHNIQUES FOR PROMPT ENGINEERING

INTRODUCTION TO ADVANCED CUSTOMIZATION

Advanced customization techniques in prompt engineering involve tailoring AI models to meet specific requirements and optimize performance for particular tasks or user preferences. This chapter explores sophisticated approaches such as prompt chaining, prompt tuning, and the use of auxiliary data to enhance the functionality and effectiveness of AI systems.

PROMPT CHAINING

Overview of Prompt Chaining:

Prompt chaining involves linking multiple prompts in a sequence to guide the AI model through complex tasks or multi-step processes. This technique is useful for scenarios where a single prompt is insufficient to capture the entire context or required actions.

Applications:

1. **Complex Task Execution:**
   o   Breaking down complex tasks into manageable steps and chaining prompts to guide the AI through each step.
   o   Example: Using prompt chaining to conduct a detailed market analysis, with separate prompts for data collection, trend identification, and recommendation generation.
2. **Iterative Refinement:**
   o   Iteratively refining outputs by chaining prompts that build on previous responses, improving accuracy and relevance.
   o   Example: Developing a research summary by chaining prompts for data extraction, initial summary, and detailed analysis.

Implementation:

python
   code
Example of implementing prompt chaining for a market

analysis task

```
initial_prompt = "Collect data on the latest market trends in the technology sector."
input_ids = tokenizer.encode(initial_prompt, return_tensors='pt')
output = model.generate(input_ids, max_length=150, num_return_sequences=1)
data_summary = tokenizer.decode(output[0], skip_special_tokens=True)

follow_up_prompt = f"Based on the data collected: {data_summary}, identify the top three emerging trends."
input_ids = tokenizer.encode(follow_up_prompt, return_tensors='pt')
output = model.generate(input_ids, max_length=150, num_return_sequences=1)
trend_analysis = tokenizer.decode(output[0], skip_special_tokens=True)

final_prompt = f"Considering the trends identified: {trend_analysis}, provide strategic recommendations for technology companies."
input_ids = tokenizer.encode(final_prompt, return_tensors='pt')
output = model.generate(input_ids, max_length=150, num_return_sequences=1)
recommendations = tokenizer.decode(output[0], skip_special_tokens=True)

print(f"Market Analysis Recommendations: {recommendations}")
```

PROMPT TUNING

Overview of Prompt Tuning:

Prompt tuning involves fine-tuning prompts to optimize the AI model's performance for specific tasks. This process can involve adjusting the wording, structure, and context of prompts to achieve better results.

Applications:

1. **Task-Specific Optimization:**
   o   Tuning prompts to improve the model's performance on particular tasks or datasets.
   o   Example: Refining prompts for a customer support chatbot to enhance response accuracy and customer satisfaction.
2. **Performance Enhancement:**
   o   Iteratively adjusting prompts based on performance metrics and user feedback to maximize effectiveness.
   o   Example: Tuning prompts for an AI writing assistant to improve the coherence and relevance of generated content.

Implementation:

python
  code
```
# Example of prompt tuning for a customer support chatbot
initial_prompt = "How can I assist you today?"
responses = [
    "I need help with my order.",
    "Can you provide information on your return policy?",
```

```
    "I'm having trouble with my account."
]
```

```python
# Function to simulate user feedback and adjust prompts
def tune_prompt(prompt, feedback):
    # Adjust the prompt based on feedback (simplified example)
    if feedback == "unclear":
        prompt += " Please provide more details so I can assist you better."
    elif feedback == "too detailed":
        prompt = "How can I assist you with your specific issue?"
    return prompt
```

```python
# Simulate tuning process
for response in responses:
    feedback = input(f"Feedback on response '{response}': ")
    tuned_prompt = tune_prompt(initial_prompt, feedback)
    print(f"Tuned Prompt: {tuned_prompt}")
```

UTILIZING
AUXILIARY DATA

Overview of Auxiliary Data:

Auxiliary data refers to additional information or datasets that can be used to enhance the context and accuracy of AI model responses. This technique involves integrating supplementary data sources to provide a richer and more informative context for prompts.

Applications:

1. **Contextual Enrichment:**
   o   Enhancing prompts with auxiliary data to provide a more comprehensive context, improving the relevance and accuracy of responses.
   o   Example: Using historical sales data and market forecasts to enrich prompts for a sales prediction model.
2. **Data-Driven Insights:**
   o   Leveraging auxiliary data to generate more informed and data-driven responses for analytical tasks.
   o   Example: Incorporating economic indicators and industry reports to support financial analysis prompts.

Implementation:

python

code

```
# Example of utilizing auxiliary data for a sales prediction
model
auxiliary_data = {
    "historical_sales": "Historical sales data shows a steady
increase over the past five years.",
    "market_forecast": "Market forecasts predict a 10% growth
in the technology sector next year."
}

# Enrich the prompt with auxiliary data
enriched_prompt = (
    f"Given the following information:\n"
    f"1. {auxiliary_data['historical_sales']}\n"
    f"2. {auxiliary_data['market_forecast']}\n"
    "Provide sales predictions for the upcoming year."
)

input_ids = tokenizer.encode(enriched_prompt,
return_tensors='pt')
output = model.generate(input_ids, max_length=150,
num_return_sequences=1)
sales_predictions = tokenizer.decode(output[0],
skip_special_tokens=True)

print(f"Sales Predictions: {sales_predictions}")
```

CONCLUSION

Advanced customization techniques such as prompt chaining, prompt tuning, and utilizing auxiliary data enable practitioners to tailor AI models to specific tasks and optimize their performance. By mastering these techniques, practitioners can create more effective, accurate, and context-aware AI systems that deliver superior results across various applications. This chapter provided detailed insights and practical examples to guide the implementation of advanced customization techniques in prompt engineering.

CHAPTER 27:
COLLABORATIVE
PROMPT
ENGINEERING

INTRODUCTION TO COLLABORATIVE PROMPT ENGINEERING

Collaborative prompt engineering involves the joint efforts of multiple stakeholders, including developers, domain experts, and end-users, to design and optimize prompts. This approach leverages diverse perspectives and expertise to enhance the quality and relevance of AI model outputs. This chapter explores strategies and methodologies for effective collaboration in prompt engineering, highlighting the benefits and practical implementation techniques.

INVOLVING DOMAIN EXPERTS

Importance of Domain Expertise:

Domain experts provide valuable insights and knowledge specific to the field in which the AI model operates. Their involvement ensures that prompts are contextually accurate and aligned with industry standards and best practices.

Strategies for Collaboration:

1. **Expert Consultation:**
   o Engage domain experts in the prompt design process to provide guidance and feedback on the contextual relevance and accuracy of prompts.
   o Example: Collaborating with healthcare professionals to develop prompts for a medical diagnosis assistant.

2. **Workshops and Brainstorming Sessions:**
   o Organize workshops and brainstorming sessions with domain experts to gather diverse ideas and perspectives on prompt engineering.
   o Example: Hosting a workshop with financial analysts to create prompts for a financial forecasting model.

Implementation:

```python
code
# Example of involving domain experts in prompt design
```

```
def consult_domain_experts(prompt, experts):
    feedback = []
    for expert in experts:
        expert_feedback = expert.review(prompt)
        feedback.append(expert_feedback)
    return feedback

initial_prompt = "Provide a diagnosis based on the following symptoms: fever, cough, and shortness of breath."
healthcare_experts = [doctor_1, doctor_2, nurse_1]

# Collect feedback from domain experts
expert_feedback = consult_domain_experts(initial_prompt, healthcare_experts)
print(f"Expert Feedback: {expert_feedback}")
```

USER-CENTRIC
DESIGN

Importance of User Involvement:

Involving end-users in the prompt engineering process ensures that the prompts are user-friendly, relevant, and effective in addressing their needs. User-centric design focuses on creating prompts that enhance the user experience and satisfaction.

Strategies for Collaboration:

1. **User Testing and Feedback:**
   o   Conduct user testing sessions to gather feedback on the usability and effectiveness of prompts.
   o   Example: Testing prompts with customer support agents to refine a chatbot's responses.
2. **Iterative Design Process:**
   o   Implement an iterative design process that incorporates user feedback into successive versions of prompts.
   o   Example: Using user feedback to iteratively improve prompts for an AI writing assistant.

Implementation:

python
   code
```
# Example of user-centric design for prompt engineering
def gather_user_feedback(prompt, users):
    feedback = []
```

```
for user in users:
    user_feedback = user.test(prompt)
    feedback.append(user_feedback)
return feedback

initial_prompt = "How can I assist you today?"
customer_support_agents = [agent_1, agent_2, agent_3]

# Collect feedback from end-users
user_feedback    =    gather_user_feedback(initial_prompt,
customer_support_agents)
print(f"User Feedback: {user_feedback}")

# Iteratively refine the prompt based on feedback
refined_prompt = initial_prompt
for feedback in user_feedback:
    refined_prompt                                          =
refine_prompt_based_on_feedback(refined_prompt, feedback)
print(f"Refined Prompt: {refined_prompt}")
```

COLLABORATIVE PLATFORMS AND TOOLS

Overview of Collaborative Tools:

Collaborative platforms and tools facilitate effective communication, coordination, and collaboration among stakeholders in the prompt engineering process. These tools support various activities such as feedback collection, version control, and project management.

Examples of Collaborative Tools:

1. **Project Management Software:**
   o   Tools such as Asana, Trello, and Jira help manage tasks, track progress, and coordinate efforts among team members.
   o   Example: Using Trello to organize and manage the prompt design process for an AI project.
2. **Version Control Systems:**
   o   Systems like Git and GitHub enable collaborative development and version control, ensuring that changes to prompts are tracked and managed effectively.
   o   Example: Using GitHub to collaborate on prompt development, allowing multiple contributors to work on the same project.

Implementation:

python
    code

```python
# Example of using collaborative tools for prompt engineering
import github

# Initialize GitHub repository for prompt engineering project
repo  =  github.Github().get_repo('organization/prompt-engineering')

# Add and commit initial prompt
with open('prompt.txt', 'w') as f:
    f.write("Provide a summary of the latest research on climate change.")
repo.create_file('prompt.txt', 'Initial prompt', f.read())

# Collaborate on prompt development
def update_prompt_file(prompt, message):
    with open('prompt.txt', 'w') as f:
        f.write(prompt)
    repo.update_file('prompt.txt',        message,        f.read(),
repo.get_contents('prompt.txt').sha)

# Example collaboration update
updated_prompt = "Provide a detailed summary of the latest research on climate change, including key findings and recommendations."
update_prompt_file(updated_prompt, 'Updated prompt for detailed summary')
```

BENEFITS OF COLLABORATIVE PROMPT ENGINEERING

Enhanced Quality and Relevance:

Collaborative prompt engineering leverages diverse expertise and perspectives, resulting in higher-quality and more relevant prompts that better meet the needs of the target audience.

Improved User Satisfaction:

By involving end-users in the design process, prompts are more likely to align with user preferences and requirements, leading to increased satisfaction and engagement.

Faster Iteration and Innovation:

Collaborative efforts enable faster iteration and innovation, as stakeholders can quickly identify issues, propose solutions, and refine prompts based on collective input.

CONCLUSION

Collaborative prompt engineering is a powerful approach that harnesses the collective expertise and perspectives of multiple stakeholders to design and optimize prompts. By involving domain experts, end-users, and utilizing collaborative tools, practitioners can enhance the quality, relevance, and effectiveness of AI model outputs. This chapter provided strategies, methodologies, and practical examples to guide the implementation of collaborative prompt engineering, highlighting its benefits and potential impact on AI-driven interactions.

CHAPTER 28: CASE STUDIES IN PROMPT ENGINEERING

INTRODUCTION TO CASE STUDIES

Case studies provide valuable insights into the practical application of prompt engineering techniques across various domains. By examining real-world examples, practitioners can learn from successful implementations, understand challenges, and gain inspiration for their own projects. This chapter presents detailed case studies that highlight different aspects of prompt engineering, showcasing innovative solutions and best practices.

CASE STUDY 1: HEALTHCARE CHATBOT FOR PATIENT TRIAGE

Overview:

A healthcare organization developed an AI-powered chatbot to assist with patient triage, providing preliminary assessments and directing patients to appropriate care based on their symptoms.

Objectives:

- Improve patient access to healthcare services.
- Reduce the workload on healthcare professionals.
- Ensure accurate and timely patient triage.

Approach:

1. **Domain Expert Collaboration:**
   o   Engaged healthcare professionals to design prompts that accurately capture patient symptoms and medical history.
   o   Example Prompt: "Please describe your symptoms, including any pain, fever, or breathing difficulties."
2. **Iterative Testing and Refinement:**
   o   Conducted user testing with patients to gather feedback on the chatbot's responses and usability.

o   Iteratively refined prompts based on user feedback to enhance clarity and relevance.

3. **Integration with Healthcare Systems:**

o   Integrated the chatbot with electronic health records (EHR) systems to provide context-aware prompts and recommendations.

o   Example Prompt: "Based on your medical history of asthma, do you have any difficulty breathing?"

Results:

- The chatbot successfully triaged a large number of patients, providing accurate recommendations and reducing the burden on healthcare professionals.
- Patient feedback indicated high satisfaction with the chatbot's responsiveness and accuracy.
- The iterative refinement process led to significant improvements in prompt design and user experience.

Lessons Learned:

- Collaboration with domain experts is crucial for designing accurate and contextually relevant prompts.
- User testing and feedback are essential for refining prompts and improving usability.
- Integration with existing systems enhances the chatbot's effectiveness and provides richer context for prompts.

CASE STUDY 2: FINANCIAL ANALYSIS ASSISTANT

Overview:

A financial services firm developed an AI assistant to support financial analysts in generating reports, conducting market analysis, and providing investment recommendations.

Objectives:

- Enhance the efficiency and accuracy of financial analysis.
- Provide real-time insights and recommendations to analysts.
- Improve the overall quality of financial reports.

Approach:

1. **Utilizing Auxiliary Data:**
   o Integrated auxiliary data sources such as market indices, economic indicators, and historical financial data to enrich prompts.
   o Example Prompt: "Analyze the impact of recent interest rate changes on the technology sector, considering historical trends and market forecasts."
2. **Advanced Customization Techniques:**
   o Employed prompt tuning to optimize prompts for specific analysis tasks and datasets.
   o Example Prompt: "Provide a detailed analysis

of the quarterly earnings report for Company X, highlighting key financial metrics and trends."

3. **Continuous Feedback and Improvement:**
   o Implemented a continuous feedback loop with financial analysts to refine prompts and improve the AI assistant's performance.
   o Example Prompt: "Based on feedback from the analysis team, revise the prompt to focus more on cash flow and profitability metrics."

Results:

- The AI assistant significantly improved the efficiency and accuracy of financial analysis, enabling analysts to focus on higher-level strategic tasks.
- Analysts reported increased satisfaction with the quality and relevance of the AI-generated reports.
- Continuous feedback and prompt refinement led to ongoing improvements in the assistant's performance.

Lessons Learned:

- Leveraging auxiliary data enhances the contextual richness and accuracy of prompts.
- Prompt tuning and customization are essential for optimizing performance for specific tasks and datasets.
- Continuous feedback and iterative improvement are key to maintaining high-quality AI outputs.

CASE STUDY 3: EDUCATIONAL AI TUTOR

Overview:

An educational technology company developed an AI tutor to provide personalized learning experiences for students, offering real-time feedback and customized lesson plans.

Objectives:

- Personalize learning experiences to meet individual student needs.
- Provide real-time feedback and support to enhance student learning.
- Improve student engagement and learning outcomes.

Approach:

1. **User-Centric Design:**
   - Involved teachers and students in the prompt design process to ensure prompts were user-friendly and effective.
   - Example Prompt: "Based on your recent performance, let's review the key concepts in algebra. Can you solve this equation?"
2. **Adaptive Learning Algorithms:**
   - Implemented adaptive learning algorithms to adjust prompts based on student progress and

performance.
o   Example Prompt: "You've mastered basic algebra. Let's move on to more advanced problems. Can you solve this quadratic equation?"
3. **Interactive and Engaging Prompts:**
o   Designed interactive and engaging prompts to maintain student interest and motivation.
o   Example Prompt: "Great job! Now let's apply what you've learned to a real-world scenario. How would you solve this problem?"

Results:

- The AI tutor successfully personalized learning experiences, leading to improved student engagement and learning outcomes.
- Teachers reported positive feedback on the AI tutor's ability to provide real-time support and adapt to individual student needs.
- Students found the interactive prompts engaging and helpful in understanding complex concepts.

Lessons Learned:

- User-centric design ensures prompts are effective and user-friendly, enhancing the overall learning experience.
- Adaptive learning algorithms enable personalized learning and continuous improvement based on student performance.
- Interactive and engaging prompts maintain student interest and motivation, leading to better learning outcomes.

CONCLUSION

These case studies highlight the practical application of prompt engineering techniques across various domains, showcasing innovative solutions and best practices. By learning from these examples, practitioners can gain valuable insights into the challenges and successes of prompt engineering, applying these lessons to their own projects to achieve superior results. This chapter provided detailed case studies that demonstrate the potential and impact of effective prompt engineering, inspiring practitioners to continue innovating and refining their approaches.

CHAPTER 29: BEST PRACTICES FOR EFFECTIVE PROMPT ENGINEERING

INTRODUCTION TO BEST PRACTICES

Effective prompt engineering requires a systematic and thoughtful approach to designing, testing, and refining prompts. By following best practices, practitioners can enhance the quality, relevance, and impact of AI model outputs. This chapter outlines key best practices for effective prompt engineering, providing practical guidance and strategies for success.

UNDERSTAND THE DOMAIN AND CONTEXT

Importance of Domain Knowledge:

A deep understanding of the domain and context in which the AI model operates is crucial for designing accurate and relevant prompts. Domain knowledge ensures that prompts align with industry standards, user expectations, and specific task requirements.

Best Practices:

1. **Engage with Domain Experts:**
   o   Collaborate with domain experts to gain insights into the specific needs and challenges of the field.
   o   Example: Working with legal professionals to design prompts for a legal research assistant.
2. **Conduct Thorough Research:**
   o   Conduct comprehensive research to understand the domain's terminology, best practices, and common use cases.
   o   Example: Studying medical literature to inform the design of prompts for a healthcare chatbot.

DESIGN CLEAR AND SPECIFIC PROMPTS

Importance of Clarity and Specificity:

Clear and specific prompts guide the AI model to generate accurate and relevant responses, reducing ambiguity and improving overall performance. Well-designed prompts provide precise instructions and context to the model.

Best Practices:

1. **Use Simple and Precise Language:**
   o   Avoid complex or ambiguous language in prompts, ensuring that instructions are easy to understand.
   o   Example: "Describe the process of photosynthesis in plants."
2. **Provide Sufficient Context:**
   o   Include relevant context and background information in prompts to guide the model's responses.
   o   Example: "Given the patient's medical history of diabetes, suggest appropriate dietary recommendations."

TEST AND VALIDATE PROMPTS

Importance of Testing and Validation:

Testing and validating prompts is essential to ensure their effectiveness and accuracy. This process involves evaluating the model's responses to identify issues and refine prompts based on feedback and performance metrics.

Best Practices:

1. **Conduct User Testing:**
   - Involve end-users in testing prompts to gather feedback on their usability and relevance.
   - Example: Testing prompts with customer support agents to refine a chatbot's responses.
2. **Implement Automated Validation:**
   - Use automated validation techniques to evaluate the model's performance on specific prompts, identifying areas for improvement.
   - Example: Running unit tests to verify the accuracy of responses to predefined prompts.

CONTINUOUSLY IMPROVE AND REFINE PROMPTS

Importance of Continuous Improvement:

Continuous improvement and refinement of prompts ensure that AI models remain effective and relevant over time. This process involves iteratively updating prompts based on user feedback, performance data, and changing requirements.

Best Practices:

1. **Gather and Incorporate Feedback:**
   o   Collect feedback from users and stakeholders to identify issues and areas for improvement in prompts.
   o   Example: Using user feedback to refine prompts for an AI writing assistant.
2. **Monitor Performance Metrics:**
   o   Regularly monitor key performance metrics to track the effectiveness of prompts and identify trends or anomalies.
   o   Example: Tracking accuracy, response time, and user satisfaction metrics for a prompt-based model.

ENSURE ETHICAL AND FAIR AI

Importance of Ethical and Fair AI:

Ensuring that AI models operate ethically and fairly is critical for building trust and avoiding bias or discrimination. Ethical prompt engineering involves designing prompts that promote fairness, transparency, and accountability.

Best Practices:

1. **Address Bias and Fairness:**
   o   Implement strategies to identify and mitigate biases in prompts and model outputs, ensuring fairness and inclusivity.
   o   Example: Using fairness metrics to evaluate the performance of prompts across different demographic groups.
2. **Maintain Transparency and Accountability:**
   o   Ensure transparency in AI operations by providing explanations for model decisions and maintaining accountability for AI-driven outcomes.
   o   Example: Implementing explainable AI techniques to make model outputs understandable and justifiable.

LEVERAGE ADVANCED TECHNIQUES AND TECHNOLOGIES

Importance of Advanced Techniques:

Leveraging advanced techniques and technologies can enhance the effectiveness and efficiency of prompt engineering. These approaches enable practitioners to optimize prompts for specific tasks and achieve superior results.

Best Practices:

1. **Use Advanced Customization:**
   o   Employ advanced customization techniques such as prompt chaining, tuning, and auxiliary data integration to tailor prompts for specific requirements.
   o   Example: Using prompt chaining to guide the AI model through complex multi-step processes.
2. **Explore Cutting-Edge Technologies:**
   o   Integrate cutting-edge technologies such as quantum computing, federated learning, and edge AI to enhance the performance and scalability of prompt-based models.
   o   Example: Using federated learning to train prompt-

based models on decentralized data while preserving privacy.

CONCLUSION

Effective prompt engineering requires a systematic approach that combines domain knowledge, clear and specific design, rigorous testing and validation, continuous improvement, ethical considerations, and advanced techniques. By following these best practices, practitioners can enhance the quality, relevance, and impact of AI model outputs, creating more effective and reliable AI-driven interactions. This chapter provided practical guidance and strategies for success, empowering practitioners to master the art and science of prompt engineering.

CHAPTER 30: THE FUTURE OF PROMPT ENGINEERING

INTRODUCTION TO THE FUTURE OF PROMPT ENGINEERING

As we conclude this comprehensive guide, it's essential to look towards the future and explore the potential advancements and opportunities in prompt engineering. The field is evolving rapidly, driven by technological innovations, changing user needs, and ongoing research. This chapter discusses emerging trends, future applications, and the evolving landscape of prompt engineering.

EMERGING TRENDS IN PROMPT ENGINEERING

Key Emerging Trends:

1. **Adaptive and Context-Aware Prompts:**
   - AI models are increasingly becoming adaptive and context-aware, enabling them to tailor prompts based on real-time user interactions and environmental factors.
   - Example: Virtual assistants that adjust prompts dynamically based on user preferences, location, and past interactions.

2. **Multimodal and Interactive Prompts:**
   - The integration of multimodal data (text, images, audio, video) is enhancing the richness and interactivity of AI-driven prompts.
   - Example: AI systems that use voice and visual inputs to generate contextually appropriate and engaging prompts.

3. **Ethical and Responsible AI:**
   - There is a growing focus on ensuring ethical and responsible AI practices, with prompt engineering playing a critical role in addressing bias, fairness, and transparency.
   - Example: Developing frameworks and guidelines for ethical prompt engineering that promote inclusivity

and accountability.

FUTURE APPLICATIONS OF PROMPT ENGINEERING

Potential Future Applications:

1. **Healthcare and Personalized Medicine:**
   o   AI-driven prompts will play a significant role in personalized medicine, guiding patients through tailored treatment plans and providing real-time health insights.
   o   Example: AI systems that generate prompts to support personalized health management, from diagnostics to ongoing care.

2. **Education and Lifelong Learning:**
   o   Prompt engineering will continue to transform education by providing personalized learning experiences, real-time feedback, and adaptive lesson plans.
   o   Example: AI tutors that generate prompts to support individualized learning paths, ensuring students achieve their full potential.

3. **Business and Industry:**
   o   AI-driven prompts will drive innovation in business and industry, enhancing decision-making, optimizing operations, and improving customer

engagement.

o   Example: AI-powered business intelligence tools that generate prompts to identify market trends, optimize supply chains, and forecast demand.

RESEARCH DIRECTIONS IN PROMPT ENGINEERING

Areas of Ongoing and Future Research:

1. **Advanced Natural Language Understanding:**
   - Research is focusing on improving the natural language understanding capabilities of AI models, enabling them to handle more complex and nuanced prompts.
   - Example: Developing models that can comprehend and generate responses to ambiguous, sarcastic, or context-dependent prompts.
2. **Zero-Shot and Few-Shot Learning:**
   - Advances in zero-shot and few-shot learning techniques are enabling AI models to generate relevant responses to new and unseen prompts with minimal training data.
   - Example: Training prompt-based models to quickly adapt to new languages, domains, or tasks with limited data.
3. **Human-AI Collaboration:**
   - Research is exploring how to enhance human-AI collaboration through improved prompt engineering, enabling more effective and seamless

interactions.
- o   Example: Studying the impact of different prompt designs on user satisfaction, engagement, and productivity in collaborative tasks.

PREPARING FOR THE FUTURE

Steps to Stay Ahead:

1. **Continuous Learning and Adaptation:**
   o Stay updated with the latest research, trends, and advancements in prompt engineering and related fields.
   o Example: Participating in conferences, workshops, and online courses on AI and prompt engineering.
2. **Innovation and Experimentation:**
   o Foster a culture of innovation and experimentation within your organization or practice, encouraging the exploration of new ideas and approaches.
   o Example: Setting up dedicated innovation labs to experiment with cutting-edge prompt engineering techniques and applications.
3. **Ethical Considerations:**
   o Prioritize ethical considerations in all prompt engineering endeavors, ensuring that AI systems are fair, transparent, and accountable.
   o Example: Developing and adhering to ethical guidelines and standards for prompt engineering practices.

CONCLUSION

The future of prompt engineering is filled with exciting opportunities and challenges. By embracing emerging trends, ongoing research, and ethical considerations, practitioners can continue to innovate and push the boundaries of what is possible with AI-driven interactions. This chapter provided a forward-looking perspective on the future of prompt engineering, offering insights and recommendations to guide practitioners in their ongoing journey of mastery and innovation.

This concludes the comprehensive guide on prompt engineering. By following the principles, strategies, and best practices outlined in this book, developers, researchers, and NLP enthusiasts can master the art and science of prompt engineering, creating effective, ethical, and innovative AI systems that drive positive impact across various domains.

CHAPTER 31: PRACTICAL TOOLS AND FRAMEWORKS FOR PROMPT ENGINEERING

INTRODUCTION TO TOOLS AND FRAMEWORKS

Leveraging the right tools and frameworks is essential for effective prompt engineering. These resources streamline the design, testing, and deployment of prompts, enabling practitioners to work more efficiently and achieve superior results. This chapter provides an overview of practical tools and frameworks that support various aspects of prompt engineering.

NATURAL LANGUAGE PROCESSING LIBRARIES

Overview of NLP Libraries:

Natural Language Processing (NLP) libraries provide essential tools and pre-trained models for text processing, analysis, and generation. They facilitate prompt engineering by offering built-in functionalities and simplifying complex tasks.

Key NLP Libraries:

1. **Transformers by Hugging Face:**
   o   The Transformers library offers state-of-the-art pre-trained models for various NLP tasks, including text generation, translation, summarization, and more.
   o   Example: Using the GPT-3 model for generating contextually relevant responses to prompts.
2. **SpaCy:**
   o   SpaCy is a fast and robust NLP library with support for tokenization, part-of-speech tagging, named entity recognition, and more.
   o   Example: Using SpaCy for text preprocessing and entity extraction to enhance prompt context.
3. **NLTK (Natural Language Toolkit):**
   o   NLTK provides a comprehensive suite of libraries and tools for text processing, including tokenization, stemming, and sentiment analysis.

○   Example: Using NLTK to preprocess text data and analyze sentiment for prompt tuning.

Implementation:

python
 code

```
# Example of using the Transformers library by Hugging Face
from transformers import GPT3Tokenizer, GPT3LMHeadModel

# Load pre-trained GPT-3 model and tokenizer
tokenizer = GPT3Tokenizer.from_pretrained('gpt3')
model = GPT3LMHeadModel.from_pretrained('gpt3')

# Generate response based on a prompt
prompt = "What are the benefits of renewable energy?"
input_ids = tokenizer.encode(prompt, return_tensors='pt')
output = model.generate(input_ids, max_length=100, num_return_sequences=1)
response = tokenizer.decode(output[0], skip_special_tokens=True)

print(f"Generated Response: {response}")
```

INTEGRATED DEVELOPMENT ENVIRONMENTS (IDES) AND NOTEBOOKS

Overview of IDEs and Notebooks:

Integrated Development Environments (IDEs) and interactive notebooks provide a conducive environment for developing, testing, and refining prompts. They offer features such as code completion, debugging, and visualization tools that enhance the development process.

Popular IDEs and Notebooks:

1. **Jupyter Notebook:**
   - Jupyter Notebook is an open-source web application that allows for interactive coding, data visualization, and narrative documentation.
   - Example: Using Jupyter Notebook to iteratively develop and test prompts with real-time feedback and visualization.
2. **PyCharm:**
   - PyCharm is a powerful IDE for Python development, offering advanced features such as code completion,

debugging, and version control integration.

o   Example: Using PyCharm to manage complex prompt engineering projects with robust debugging and project management tools.

3. **VS Code (Visual Studio Code):**

o   VS Code is a lightweight yet powerful code editor with support for various programming languages, extensions, and integrated terminal.

o   Example: Using VS Code to develop, test, and deploy prompt-based models with integrated support for Git and other extensions.

Implementation:

python
  code

```
# Example of using Jupyter Notebook for prompt engineering
# Install Jupyter Notebook if not already installed
!pip install notebook

# Start a Jupyter Notebook session
!jupyter notebook
```

CLOUD PLATFORMS AND SERVICES

Overview of Cloud Platforms:

Cloud platforms provide scalable infrastructure and services for deploying and managing AI models. They offer various tools for data storage, processing, and model deployment, making them ideal for large-scale prompt engineering projects.

Key Cloud Platforms:

1. **Amazon Web Services (AWS):**
   o   AWS offers a wide range of cloud services, including computing, storage, machine learning, and analytics.
   o   Example: Using AWS SageMaker for training and deploying prompt-based models in a scalable and managed environment.

2. **Google Cloud Platform (GCP):**
   o   GCP provides cloud services for computing, storage, machine learning, and data analytics, with a focus on AI and data-driven applications.
   o   Example: Using Google Cloud AI Platform for developing, training, and deploying prompt-based models.

3. **Microsoft Azure:**
   o   Azure offers cloud services for computing, storage, machine learning, and more, with robust support for

enterprise applications.

o   Example: Using Azure Machine Learning for building and deploying prompt-based models with integrated monitoring and management tools.

Implementation:

python
   code

```
# Example of deploying a prompt-based model on AWS SageMaker
import sagemaker
from sagemaker.pytorch import PyTorchModel

# Define the S3 bucket and role for SageMaker
s3_bucket = 's3://my-bucket'
role = 'arn:aws:iam::123456789012:role/SageMakerRole'

# Create a PyTorch model
model        =        PyTorchModel(model_data=f'{s3_bucket}/model.tar.gz',
            role=role,
            entry_point='inference.py',
            framework_version='1.6.0')

# Deploy the model
predictor    =    model.deploy(instance_type='ml.m4.xlarge',
initial_instance_count=1)

# Use the deployed model for inference
response = predictor.predict('What are the benefits of cloud computing?')
print(f"Model Response: {response}")
```

VERSION CONTROL AND COLLABORATION TOOLS

Overview of Version Control:

Version control systems help manage changes to code and documents, facilitating collaboration among multiple contributors. They ensure that all changes are tracked and can be reverted if necessary, making them essential for collaborative prompt engineering projects.

Popular Version Control Systems:

1. **Git:**
   o   Git is a distributed version control system that tracks changes in source code during software development.
   o   Example: Using Git to manage changes to prompt engineering code and collaborate with team members.
2. **GitHub:**
   o   GitHub is a web-based platform that uses Git for version control and offers additional collaboration features such as issue tracking and pull requests.
   o   Example: Using GitHub to collaborate on prompt engineering projects, track issues, and review code

changes.

Implementation:

python
  code

```
# Example of using Git for version control in prompt
engineering
# Initialize a Git repository
!git init

# Add and commit files
!git add .
!git commit -m "Initial commit"

# Push to a remote repository on GitHub
!git remote add origin https://github.com/username/prompt-
engineering.git
!git push -u origin master
```

DATA ANNOTATION AND LABELING TOOLS

Overview of Data Annotation:

Data annotation and labeling tools facilitate the creation of labeled datasets, which are essential for training and evaluating AI models. These tools support various types of annotations, including text, image, audio, and video.

Key Data Annotation Tools:

1. **Labelbox:**
   o   Labelbox is a data annotation platform that supports various annotation types and integrates with machine learning workflows.
   o   Example: Using Labelbox to annotate text data for training prompt-based models.
2. **Amazon SageMaker Ground Truth:**
   o   SageMaker Ground Truth provides tools for building high-quality labeled datasets, offering automated labeling features to reduce annotation costs.
   o   Example: Using Ground Truth to create labeled datasets for prompt engineering projects.
3. **Prodigy:**
   o   Prodigy is an annotation tool designed for NLP tasks, supporting active learning workflows to improve annotation efficiency.

- o Example: Using Prodigy to annotate text data and iteratively improve prompt-based models.

Implementation:

python
  code

```
# Example of using Prodigy for data annotation
# Install Prodigy if not already installed
!pip install prodigy

# Start a Prodigy annotation session
!prodigy ner.manual my_dataset en_core_web_sm "path/to/
text/files"
```

CONCLUSION

Leveraging practical tools and frameworks is essential for effective prompt engineering. This chapter provided an overview of key resources, including NLP libraries, IDEs, cloud platforms, version control systems, and data annotation tools, to support various aspects of prompt engineering. By utilizing these tools, practitioners can streamline the development, testing, and deployment of prompts, achieving superior results in their AI-driven interactions.

CHAPTER 32: ADVANCED EVALUATION METRICS FOR PROMPT ENGINEERING

INTRODUCTION TO EVALUATION METRICS

Evaluating the effectiveness of prompts is crucial for ensuring that AI models generate accurate, relevant, and useful responses. Advanced evaluation metrics provide a comprehensive understanding of model performance, guiding prompt refinement and optimization. This chapter explores various advanced evaluation metrics for prompt engineering, including both quantitative and qualitative approaches.

QUANTITATIVE METRICS

Overview of Quantitative Metrics:

Quantitative metrics provide objective measures of model performance, enabling practitioners to assess the accuracy, relevance, and coherence of responses. These metrics are essential for evaluating the effectiveness of prompts and identifying areas for improvement.

Key Quantitative Metrics:

1. **BLEU Score:**
   - The BLEU (Bilingual Evaluation Understudy) score measures the overlap between generated responses and reference texts, evaluating the precision of n-grams.
   - Example: Using BLEU score to evaluate the accuracy of responses generated by a translation model.
2. **ROUGE Score:**
   - The ROUGE (Recall-Oriented Understudy for Gisting Evaluation) score measures the overlap between generated responses and reference texts, focusing on recall of n-grams.
   - Example: Using ROUGE score to assess the relevance of summaries generated by a text summarization model.
3. **Perplexity:**
   - Perplexity measures how well a language model

predicts a sample, with lower perplexity indicating better performance.

o   Example: Using perplexity to evaluate the fluency and coherence of responses generated by a language model.

Implementation:

python
  code

```
# Example of calculating BLEU and ROUGE scores for prompt
evaluation
from nltk.translate.bleu_score import sentence_bleu
from rouge import Rouge

# Define reference and generated responses
reference = "The benefits of renewable energy include reducing
greenhouse gas emissions and decreasing dependence on
fossil fuels."
generated = "Renewable energy helps reduce greenhouse gas
emissions and reliance on fossil fuels."

# Calculate BLEU score
bleu_score           =              sentence_bleu([reference.split()],
generated.split())
print(f"BLEU Score: {bleu_score}")

# Calculate ROUGE score
rouge = Rouge()
rouge_score = rouge.get_scores(generated, reference)
print(f"ROUGE Score: {rouge_score}")
```

QUALITATIVE METRICS

Overview of Qualitative Metrics:

Qualitative metrics provide subjective assessments of model performance, focusing on the quality, coherence, and relevance of responses. These metrics involve human evaluation and feedback, offering valuable insights into the user experience.

Key Qualitative Metrics:

1. **Human Evaluation:**
   - Human evaluators assess the quality, coherence, and relevance of generated responses, providing scores or qualitative feedback.
   - Example: Conducting user studies to evaluate the effectiveness of prompts for a customer support chatbot.
2. **Usability Testing:**
   - Usability testing involves observing users as they interact with the AI system, identifying issues and gathering feedback on the user experience.
   - Example: Conducting usability tests to refine prompts for an AI writing assistant.
3. **User Satisfaction Surveys:**
   - Surveys collect feedback from users on their satisfaction with the AI system's responses, providing insights into areas for improvement.

○ Example: Using surveys to gather user feedback on the relevance and accuracy of prompts in a virtual assistant.

Implementation:

python
code

```
# Example of conducting human evaluation for prompt
evaluation
def    human_evaluation(prompt,    generated_response,
reference_response):
    # Simulate human evaluation process
    print(f"Prompt: {prompt}")
    print(f"Generated Response: {generated_response}")
    print(f"Reference Response: {reference_response}")
    rating = input("Rate the quality of the generated response
(1-5): ")
    comments = input("Provide any additional feedback: ")
    return rating, comments

# Define prompt and responses
prompt = "What are the benefits of renewable energy?"
generated_response = "Renewable energy helps reduce
greenhouse gas emissions and reliance on fossil fuels."
reference_response = "The benefits of renewable energy
include reducing greenhouse gas emissions and decreasing
dependence on fossil fuels."

# Conduct human evaluation
rating,    comments    =    human_evaluation(prompt,
generated_response, reference_response)
print(f"Human Evaluation Rating: {rating}")
print(f"Human Evaluation Comments: {comments}")
```

COMBINED METRICS

Overview of Combined Metrics:

Combined metrics integrate both quantitative and qualitative approaches, providing a holistic assessment of model performance. These metrics leverage the strengths of each approach to offer comprehensive insights into the effectiveness of prompts.

Key Combined Metrics:

1. **F1 Score:**
   - The F1 score combines precision and recall, providing a balanced measure of accuracy and relevance.
   - Example: Using the F1 score to evaluate the overall performance of a text classification model.
2. **User-Centric Metrics:**
   - User-centric metrics combine quantitative performance measures with user feedback, offering a balanced view of technical accuracy and user satisfaction.
   - Example: Combining BLEU scores with user satisfaction ratings to evaluate the effectiveness of prompts for a translation model.

Implementation:

python
   code

```
# Example of calculating F1 score for prompt evaluation
from sklearn.metrics import f1_score
```

```
# Define reference and generated responses (binary
classification example)
reference_labels = [1, 0, 1, 1, 0]
generated_labels = [1, 0, 1, 0, 0]

# Calculate F1 score
f1 = f1_score(reference_labels, generated_labels)
print(f"F1 Score: {f1}")
```

BEST PRACTICES FOR EVALUATION

Implementing Best Practices:

1. **Use Multiple Metrics:**
   - Employ a combination of quantitative and qualitative metrics to gain a comprehensive understanding of model performance.
   - Example: Using BLEU, ROUGE, and human evaluation to assess the effectiveness of prompts for a summarization model.

2. **Iterative Evaluation:**
   - Conduct iterative evaluations, refining prompts based on feedback and performance data to achieve continuous improvement.
   - Example: Iteratively testing and refining prompts for a customer support chatbot to enhance response accuracy and relevance.

3. **Engage Diverse Evaluators:**
   - Involve diverse evaluators in the assessment process to ensure a wide range of perspectives and avoid biases.
   - Example: Conducting user studies with participants from different backgrounds to evaluate the inclusivity and fairness of prompts.

CONCLUSION

Advanced evaluation metrics provide a comprehensive framework for assessing the effectiveness of prompts in AI models. By combining quantitative and qualitative approaches, practitioners can gain valuable insights into model performance, guiding prompt refinement and optimization. This chapter provided an overview of key evaluation metrics, practical implementation examples, and best practices to support effective prompt engineering.

CHAPTER 33: ETHICAL CONSIDERATIONS IN PROMPT ENGINEERING

INTRODUCTION TO ETHICAL CONSIDERATIONS

Ensuring ethical practices in prompt engineering is essential for developing AI systems that are fair, transparent, and accountable. Ethical considerations address issues such as bias, privacy, inclusivity, and transparency, ensuring that AI models operate responsibly and respect user rights. This chapter explores key ethical considerations in prompt engineering and provides practical guidelines for ethical AI development.

ADDRESSING BIAS AND FAIRNESS

Importance of Bias Mitigation:

Bias in AI models can lead to unfair and discriminatory outcomes, impacting user trust and societal equity. Addressing bias is crucial for ensuring that AI systems operate fairly and inclusively.

Strategies for Bias Mitigation:

1. **Diverse Training Data:**
   o   Use diverse and representative datasets to train AI models, ensuring that all demographic groups are adequately represented.
   o   Example: Incorporating data from various regions, genders, and socioeconomic backgrounds in training datasets for a language model.
2. **Bias Detection and Correction:**
   o   Implement tools and techniques to detect and correct biases in model outputs, ensuring fairness and inclusivity.
   o   Example: Using fairness metrics to evaluate model performance across different demographic groups and applying corrective measures as needed.

Implementation:

python
code
Example of implementing bias detection and correction

```python
def detect_bias(prompt, model):
    input_ids = tokenizer.encode(prompt, return_tensors='pt')
    output = model.generate(input_ids, max_length=50, num_return_sequences=1)
    response = tokenizer.decode(output[0], skip_special_tokens=True)

    # Simple bias detection example
    bias_keywords = ["gender", "ethnicity", "race"]
    if any(keyword in response.lower() for keyword in bias_keywords):
        print(f"Potential Bias Detected in Response: {response}")
    else:
        print(f"Response: {response}")

prompt = "Describe a typical leader."
detect_bias(prompt, model)
```

ENSURING PRIVACY AND DATA PROTECTION

Importance of Privacy:

Protecting user privacy is critical for maintaining trust and complying with regulatory requirements. Ethical AI practices involve safeguarding user data and ensuring that privacy is respected throughout the AI development lifecycle.

Strategies for Privacy Protection:

1. **Data Anonymization:**
   o   Implement data anonymization techniques to remove personally identifiable information (PII) from datasets, protecting user privacy.
   o   Example: Anonymizing user data before using it to train prompt-based models.
2. **Compliance with Regulations:**
   o   Ensure compliance with privacy regulations such as GDPR and HIPAA, implementing measures to protect user data and provide transparency.
   o   Example: Implementing user consent mechanisms and data deletion requests in compliance with GDPR requirements.

Implementation:

python

code

```python
# Example of implementing data anonymization
import pandas as pd

# Load user data
data = pd.read_csv('user_data.csv')

# Anonymize data by removing PII
anonymized_data = data.drop(columns=['name', 'email', 'phone'])

# Save anonymized data
anonymized_data.to_csv('anonymized_user_data.csv',
index=False)
print("Data anonymization complete")
```

PROMOTING INCLUSIVITY AND ACCESSIBILITY

Importance of Inclusivity:

Ensuring that AI models are inclusive and accessible to all users is essential for promoting fairness and reducing digital divides. Inclusive AI practices involve designing prompts and systems that cater to diverse user needs and abilities.

Strategies for Inclusivity:

1. **Inclusive Language:**
   - Use inclusive language in prompts to ensure that all users feel respected and represented.
   - Example: Avoiding gendered language and using neutral terms in prompts.
2. **Accessibility Features:**
   - Implement accessibility features to support users with different abilities, ensuring that AI systems are usable by everyone.
   - Example: Designing prompts for screen readers and providing alternative input methods for users with disabilities.

Implementation:

python
   code

```python
# Example of using inclusive language in prompts
def generate_inclusive_prompt(prompt):
    # Replace gendered terms with neutral terms
    inclusive_prompt = prompt.replace("he", "they").replace("she", "they").replace("him", "them").replace("her", "them")
    return inclusive_prompt

prompt = "Describe how a leader can inspire his team."
inclusive_prompt = generate_inclusive_prompt(prompt)
print(f"Inclusive Prompt: {inclusive_prompt}")
```

ENSURING TRANSPARENCY AND ACCOUNTABILITY

Importance of Transparency:

Transparency in AI operations is essential for building trust and ensuring accountability. Providing clear explanations for model decisions and maintaining accountability for AI-driven outcomes are key aspects of ethical AI practices.

Strategies for Transparency:

1. **Explainable AI (XAI):**
   o   Implement explainable AI techniques to make model decisions understandable and justifiable to users.
   o   Example: Providing explanations for how a model generated a particular response to a prompt.
2. **Audit and Accountability Mechanisms:**
   o   Implement audit mechanisms to track and review AI model decisions, ensuring accountability for outcomes.
   o   Example: Maintaining logs of model outputs and decision-making processes for review and analysis.

Implementation:

python
   code

```python
# Example of implementing explainable AI (XAI) techniques
from transformers import pipeline

# Load a pre-trained model with explainability support
model = pipeline("text-classification", model="distilbert-base-uncased")

# Generate an explanation for a model decision
prompt = "Classify the sentiment of this text: 'I love this product!'"
explanation = model(prompt, return_all_scores=True)

print(f"Model Decision Explanation: {explanation}")
```

ETHICAL GUIDELINES AND FRAMEWORKS

Importance of Ethical Guidelines:

Adhering to ethical guidelines and frameworks ensures that AI development practices align with broader societal values and ethical standards. These guidelines provide a structured approach to addressing ethical considerations in AI.

Key Ethical Guidelines:

1. **AI Ethics Principles:**
   - Follow established AI ethics principles such as fairness, accountability, and transparency to guide AI development.
   - Example: Adopting principles from organizations like the AI Ethics Guidelines by the European Commission or IEEE's Ethically Aligned Design.
2. **Ethical Review Processes:**
   - Implement ethical review processes to assess the potential impact of AI systems and ensure alignment with ethical standards.
   - Example: Conducting regular ethical audits and reviews of AI projects to identify and address ethical issues.

Implementation:

python
   code
```
# Example of conducting an ethical review for an AI project
```

```
def ethical_review(prompt, model):
    # Simulate ethical review process
    print(f"Conducting ethical review for prompt: {prompt}")
    response = model(prompt)
    # Check for potential ethical issues
    ethical_issues = []
    if "bias" in response.lower():
        ethical_issues.append("Bias detected in response.")
    if "privacy" in response.lower():
        ethical_issues.append("Privacy concern detected in
response.")
    return ethical_issues

prompt = "Describe the characteristics of a typical leader."
ethical_issues = ethical_review(prompt, model)
print(f"Ethical Issues: {ethical_issues}")
```

CONCLUSION

Ethical considerations are paramount in prompt engineering, ensuring that AI systems operate responsibly, fairly, and transparently. By addressing bias, protecting privacy, promoting inclusivity, ensuring transparency, and adhering to ethical guidelines, practitioners can develop AI models that respect user rights and contribute positively to society. This chapter provided practical strategies and implementation examples to guide ethical AI development, emphasizing the importance of responsible practices in prompt engineering.

CHAPTER 34: BUILDING A COMMUNITY FOR PROMPT ENGINEERING

INTRODUCTION TO COMMUNITY BUILDING

Building a community around prompt engineering fosters collaboration, knowledge sharing, and innovation. A strong community provides a platform for practitioners to exchange ideas, share best practices, and contribute to the advancement of the field. This chapter explores strategies for building and nurturing a community for prompt engineering, highlighting the benefits and practical steps for effective community engagement.

ESTABLISHING A COMMUNITY PLATFORM

Overview of Community Platforms:

A community platform provides a central space for members to interact, share resources, and collaborate on projects. Choosing the right platform is crucial for effective community building and engagement.

Popular Community Platforms:

1. **Online Forums:**
   o   Online forums such as Reddit, Stack Overflow, and dedicated community websites offer spaces for discussions, Q&A, and resource sharing.
   o   Example: Creating a subreddit or a dedicated forum for prompt engineering topics and discussions.
2. **Social Media Groups:**
   o   Social media platforms such as LinkedIn, Facebook, and Twitter provide opportunities for creating groups and communities focused on specific interests.
   o   Example: Establishing a LinkedIn group for prompt engineering professionals to network and share insights.
3. **Collaboration Tools:**
   o   Collaboration tools such as Slack, Discord, and

Microsoft Teams offer real-time communication and collaboration features, fostering active engagement.

o   Example: Setting up a Slack workspace for prompt engineering practitioners to discuss projects, share resources, and collaborate.

Implementation:

python
   code

```python
# Example of setting up a Slack workspace for prompt
engineering
import slack_sdk

# Create a Slack client
client = slack_sdk.WebClient(token='your-slack-api-token')

# Create a channel for prompt engineering discussions
response    =    client.conversations_create(name='prompt-
engineering', is_private=False)
channel_id = response['channel']['id']

# Invite members to the channel
members = ['user1', 'user2', 'user3']
for member in members:
    client.conversations_invite(channel=channel_id,
users=member)

print("Slack workspace for prompt engineering set up
successfully")
```

ORGANIZING COMMUNITY EVENTS

Importance of Community Events:

Community events provide opportunities for members to connect, learn, and collaborate. Organizing regular events such as webinars, workshops, and hackathons fosters engagement and strengthens the community.

Types of Community Events:

1. **Webinars and Workshops:**
   - Webinars and workshops offer educational sessions on various topics related to prompt engineering, featuring expert speakers and hands-on activities.
   - Example: Hosting a webinar on advanced prompt engineering techniques with guest speakers from the industry.
2. **Hackathons and Competitions:**
   - Hackathons and competitions encourage members to collaborate on projects, solve challenges, and showcase their skills.
   - Example: Organizing a hackathon to develop innovative prompt-based AI solutions for real-world problems.
3. **Meetups and Networking Events:**
   - Meetups and networking events provide opportunities for members to connect, share experiences, and build relationships.

- o Example: Hosting a virtual meetup for prompt engineering practitioners to discuss trends and share best practices.

Implementation:

python
  code

```
# Example of organizing a webinar on advanced prompt engineering techniques
import webinar_platform_sdk

# Create a webinar event
webinar = webinar_platform_sdk.create_event(
    title='Advanced Prompt Engineering Techniques',
    description='Learn advanced techniques and best practices in prompt engineering from industry experts.',
    date='2023-09-30',
    time='10:00 AM - 12:00 PM'
)

# Invite speakers and participants
speakers = ['expert1', 'expert2']
participants = ['participant1', 'participant2', 'participant3']
webinar.invite_speakers(speakers)
webinar.invite_participants(participants)

print("Webinar on advanced prompt engineering techniques organized successfully")
```

ENCOURAGING KNOWLEDGE SHARING

Importance of Knowledge Sharing:

Knowledge sharing is crucial for community growth and innovation. Encouraging members to share their insights, experiences, and resources fosters a collaborative learning environment.

Strategies for Knowledge Sharing:

1. **Resource Libraries:**
   o   Create and maintain resource libraries with articles, tutorials, research papers, and tools related to prompt engineering.
   o   Example: Establishing an online repository of prompt engineering resources that community members can access and contribute to.
2. **Blog Posts and Articles:**
   o   Encourage members to write blog posts and articles on their experiences, projects, and best practices in prompt engineering.
   o   Example: Featuring member-written articles on a community blog or newsletter.
3. **Discussion Threads and Q&A Sessions:**
   o   Facilitate discussion threads and Q&A sessions where members can ask questions, seek advice, and

share knowledge.

o   Example: Hosting monthly Q&A sessions with experts to address community members' questions and challenges.

Implementation:

python
  code

```
# Example of creating a resource library for prompt
engineering
import os

# Create a directory for the resource library
os.makedirs('prompt_engineering_resources', exist_ok=True)

# Add resources to the library
resources = {
    'articles': ['article1.pdf', 'article2.pdf'],
    'tutorials': ['tutorial1.ipynb', 'tutorial2.ipynb'],
    'tools': ['tool1.py', 'tool2.py']
}

for category, files in resources.items():
    category_path                                    =
os.path.join('prompt_engineering_resources', category)
    os.makedirs(category_path, exist_ok=True)
    for file in files:
        # Simulate adding files to the resource library
        with open(os.path.join(category_path, file), 'w') as f:
            f.write(f"Content of {file}")

print("Resource library for prompt engineering created
successfully")
```

RECOGNIZING AND REWARDING CONTRIBUTIONS

Importance of Recognition:

Recognizing and rewarding contributions motivates members to actively participate and contribute to the community. It fosters a positive environment and encourages continuous engagement.

Strategies for Recognition:

1. **Member Spotlights:**
   o   Feature outstanding members and their contributions in community newsletters, blogs, or social media.
   o   Example: Highlighting a member's innovative project or significant contributions to community discussions.
2. **Awards and Certificates:**
   o   Offer awards and certificates for notable contributions, achievements, or participation in community events.
   o   Example: Issuing certificates of appreciation for members who present webinars or lead workshops.
3. **Incentives and Rewards:**
   o   Provide incentives and rewards such as gift cards, swag, or exclusive access to resources for active

> participation and contributions.
>
> o   Example: Offering gift cards to members who consistently share valuable insights and resources.

Implementation:

python
   code

```
# Example of issuing certificates of appreciation for
community contributions
from reportlab.lib.pagesizes import letter
from reportlab.pdfgen import canvas

def create_certificate(name, contribution):
    c       =         canvas.Canvas(f"{name}_certificate.pdf",
pagesize=letter)
    c.drawString(100, 750, f"Certificate of Appreciation")
    c.drawString(100, 725, f"Presented to: {name}")
    c.drawString(100, 700,
```

750, f"Certificate of Appreciation") c.drawString(100, 725, f"Presented to: {name}") c.drawString(100, 700, f"In recognition of their valuable contribution to the Prompt Engineering community, particularly for:") c.drawString(100, 675, contribution) c.drawString(100, 650, f"Date: {datetime.date.today()}") c.drawString(100, 625, "Signature:") c.line(150, 620, 250, 620) c.save()

CREATE A CERTIFICATE FOR A MEMBER

```
create_certificate("Jane Doe", "presenting an insightful
webinar on advanced prompt tuning techniques.")
print("Certificate of Appreciation created successfully")
```

less
  code

Building a Culture of Collaboration

Importance of Collaborative Culture:

Fostering a culture of collaboration within the community encourages members to work together, share knowledge, and support each other's growth. This collaborative spirit drives innovation and enhances the overall effectiveness of the community.

Strategies for Building Collaboration:

1. **Mentorship Programs:**
   - Establish mentorship programs where experienced members guide newcomers, sharing their expertise and providing support.
   - Example: Pairing experienced prompt engineers with new members to help them navigate challenges and develop their skills.

2. **Collaborative Projects:**

- Encourage members to collaborate on projects, sharing responsibilities and combining their strengths to achieve common goals.
- Example: Initiating a community-wide project to develop a comprehensive prompt engineering toolkit.

3. **Open Communication Channels:**
- Maintain open and inclusive communication channels where members can freely share ideas, ask questions, and provide feedback.
- Example: Setting up dedicated discussion channels in a Slack workspace for different topics related to prompt engineering.

Implementation:

```python
# Example of setting up a mentorship program
def setup_mentorship_program(mentors, mentees):
    mentorship_pairs = []
    for mentor in mentors:
        for mentee in mentees:
            if
mentee['interests'].intersection(mentor['expertise']):
                mentorship_pairs.append((mentor['name'],
mentee['name']))
                break
    return mentorship_pairs

mentors = [    {'name': 'Alice', 'expertise': {'prompt tuning',
'NLP'}},    {'name': 'Bob', 'expertise': {'data annotation', 'model
deployment'}}]

mentees = [    {'name': 'Charlie', 'interests': {'prompt tuning'}},
{'name': 'Dave', 'interests': {'data annotation'}}]

mentorship_pairs    =    setup_mentorship_program(mentors,
mentees)
print(f"Mentorship Pairs: {mentorship_pairs}")
```

CONCLUSION

Building a community for prompt engineering involves creating a collaborative platform, organizing events, encouraging knowledge sharing, recognizing contributions, and fostering a culture of collaboration. These strategies help create a vibrant and engaged community that drives innovation and supports the growth of its members. By following the guidelines and examples provided in this chapter, practitioners can effectively build and nurture a thriving prompt engineering community.

CHAPTER 35:
CONCLUSION AND
FUTURE DIRECTIONS

SUMMARY OF KEY INSIGHTS

Throughout this comprehensive guide, we have explored the various aspects of prompt engineering, from foundational concepts to advanced techniques and practical applications. Key insights from this guide include:

1. **Foundations of Prompt Engineering:**
   o Understanding the basic principles and importance of prompt engineering in AI and NLP.
   o Exploring different types of prompts and their applications.
2. **Designing Effective Prompts:**
   o Learning the principles of clear and specific prompts.
   o Techniques for designing prompts that balance guidance and creativity.
3. **Evaluating and Validating Prompts:**
   o Using metrics to assess prompt effectiveness.
   o Implementing both automated and human evaluation methods.
4. **Advanced Techniques and Customization:**
   o Utilizing advanced methods like prompt chaining, tuning, and leveraging auxiliary data.
   o Integrating cutting-edge technologies such as quantum computing, federated learning, and edge AI.
5. **Ethical Considerations:**

○   Addressing bias, ensuring privacy, promoting inclusivity, and maintaining transparency in prompt engineering.

6. **Building a Community:**

○   Establishing platforms, organizing events, encouraging knowledge sharing, and fostering collaboration to build a strong prompt engineering community.

FUTURE DIRECTIONS IN PROMPT ENGINEERING

As the field of prompt engineering continues to evolve, several future directions and emerging trends will shape its development:

1. **Adaptive and Context-Aware Prompts:**
   o   Development of AI models that dynamically adjust prompts based on real-time user interactions and contextual factors.
2. **Multimodal Integration:**
   o   Incorporation of multimodal data (text, images, audio, video) to create richer and more interactive prompts.
3. **Ethical and Responsible AI:**
   o   Continued emphasis on ethical considerations, including fairness, transparency, and accountability in prompt engineering.
4. **Zero-Shot and Few-Shot Learning:**
   o   Advances in learning techniques that enable AI models to generate relevant responses with minimal training data.
5. **Human-AI Collaboration:**
   o   Enhancing human-AI collaboration through improved prompt engineering, enabling more seamless and effective interactions.

RECOMMENDATIONS FOR PRACTITIONERS

To stay ahead in the rapidly evolving field of prompt engineering, practitioners should:

1. **Stay Informed:**
   - Keep up-to-date with the latest research, trends, and advancements in prompt engineering and related fields.
2. **Engage in Continuous Learning:**
   - Participate in conferences, workshops, and online courses to deepen knowledge and skills.
3. **Foster Innovation:**
   - Encourage a culture of experimentation and innovation within your organization or practice.
4. **Prioritize Ethics:**
   - Adhere to ethical guidelines and standards, ensuring that AI systems are fair, transparent, and accountable.
5. **Build and Nurture Community:**
   - Engage with the prompt engineering community to share knowledge, collaborate on projects, and contribute to the field's advancement.

FINAL THOUGHTS

Prompt engineering is a critical aspect of AI and NLP that drives the effectiveness and relevance of AI model interactions. By mastering the principles, strategies, and techniques outlined in this guide, practitioners can create powerful and innovative AI systems that deliver significant value across various domains. As the field continues to evolve, the opportunities for innovation and impact in prompt engineering are vast, and the journey of mastery and discovery is ongoing.

This concludes the comprehensive guide on prompt engineering. Thank you for exploring this field with us. We hope this guide serves as a valuable resource in your journey to mastering prompt engineering and leveraging its full potential in AI-driven interactions.

APPENDICES

APPENDIX A: GLOSSARY OF KEY TERMS

Adaptive Learning: A learning approach where AI models adjust their responses based on real-time feedback and context, enhancing personalization and relevance.

Bias Mitigation: Techniques used to identify, address, and reduce biases in AI models to ensure fairness and inclusivity.

Context-Aware Prompts: Prompts designed to dynamically adjust based on contextual information such as user behavior, preferences, and environmental factors.

Differential Privacy: A method of adding noise to data to protect individual privacy while preserving the overall utility of the dataset.

Explainable AI (XAI): Techniques and tools used to make AI model decisions understandable and transparent to users.

Federated Learning: A decentralized approach to machine learning where models are trained across multiple devices or servers without sharing raw data.

Few-Shot Learning: A learning technique that enables AI models to generate relevant responses or make predictions with a limited amount of training data.

Human-AI Collaboration: A collaborative approach where

humans and AI systems work together to achieve common goals, leveraging the strengths of both parties.

Inclusive Language: Language that avoids bias, stereotypes, and discriminatory terms, ensuring respect and representation for all users.

Multimodal Data: Data that includes multiple types of information such as text, images, audio, and video, providing a richer context for AI models.

Prompt Engineering: The process of designing, testing, and refining prompts to guide AI models in generating accurate and relevant responses.

Quantum Computing: A type of computing that leverages quantum mechanics principles to perform calculations at unprecedented speeds, useful for solving complex optimization problems.

Zero-Shot Learning: A learning technique where AI models can generate relevant responses or make predictions for tasks they have not been explicitly trained on.

APPENDIX B: SAMPLE PROMPTS AND USE CASES

Sample Prompts for Healthcare:

1. **Symptom Checker:**
   o   "Describe your symptoms in detail, including any pain, fever, or difficulty breathing."
   o   "Based on your symptoms, suggest possible diagnoses and recommended next steps."
2. **Medication Information:**
   o   "Provide detailed information on the medication 'Aspirin,' including its uses, dosage, and potential side effects."
3. **Dietary Recommendations:**
   o   "Given a patient with diabetes, recommend a suitable diet plan, including meal options and nutritional guidelines."

Sample Prompts for Financial Services:

1. **Market Analysis:**
   o   "Analyze the impact of recent interest rate changes on the technology sector, considering historical trends and market forecasts."
   o   "Provide a detailed analysis of the quarterly earnings report for Company X, highlighting key financial metrics and trends."

2. **Investment Recommendations:**
o   "Based on the current market conditions, suggest investment strategies for a conservative investor seeking long-term growth."
o   "Evaluate the performance of various asset classes over the past decade and recommend a diversified investment portfolio."
3. **Risk Assessment:**
o   "Assess the risk profile of a potential loan applicant based on their credit history, income, and debt-to-income ratio."
o   "Identify and explain the key risks associated with investing in emerging markets, including political and economic factors."

Sample Prompts for Education:

1. **Personalized Learning:**
o   "Based on the student's recent performance, suggest personalized learning activities to improve their understanding of algebra."
o   "Create a customized lesson plan for a high school student struggling with biology, including interactive exercises and resources."
2. **Real-Time Feedback:**
o   "Provide real-time feedback on the student's essay, focusing on grammar, coherence, and argument structure."
o   "Analyze the student's solution to a math problem and provide step-by-step guidance for correcting any mistakes."
3. **Interactive Learning:**
o   "Design an interactive quiz on the principles of physics for high school students, including multiple-choice and short-answer questions."
o   "Create a virtual lab simulation for chemistry students to explore chemical reactions and practice

safety procedures."

APPENDIX C: TOOLS AND RESOURCES

NLP Libraries and Frameworks:

1. **Transformers by Hugging Face:**
   - URL: https://huggingface.co/transformers
   - Description: State-of-the-art pre-trained models for various NLP tasks, including text generation, translation, and summarization.
2. **SpaCy:**
   - URL: https://spacy.io
   - Description: Fast and robust NLP library with support for tokenization, part-of-speech tagging, named entity recognition, and more.
3. **NLTK (Natural Language Toolkit):**
   - URL: https://www.nltk.org
   - Description: Comprehensive suite of libraries and tools for text processing, including tokenization, stemming, and sentiment analysis.

Cloud Platforms and Services:

1. **Amazon Web Services (AWS):**
   - URL: https://aws.amazon.com
   - Description: Wide range of cloud services for computing, storage, machine learning, and analytics, including AWS Sagemaker for AI model training and deployment.
2. **Google Cloud Platform (GCP):**

- o URL: https://cloud.google.com
- o Description: Cloud services for computing, storage, machine learning, and data analytics, with a focus on AI and data-driven applications.
3. **Microsoft Azure:**
- o URL: https://azure.microsoft.com
- o Description: Cloud services for computing, storage, machine learning, and more, with robust support for enterprise applications.

Version Control and Collaboration Tools:

1. **Git:**
- o URL: https://git-scm.com
- o Description: Distributed version control system that tracks changes in source code during software development.
2. **GitHub:**
- o URL: https://github.com
- o Description: Web-based platform using Git for version control, offering collaboration features such as issue tracking and pull requests.

Data Annotation and Labeling Tools:

1. **Labelbox:**
- o URL: https://labelbox.com
- o Description: Data annotation platform supporting various annotation types, integrating with machine learning workflows.
2. **Amazon SageMaker Ground Truth:**
- o URL: https://aws.amazon.com/sagemaker/groundtruth
- o Description: Tools for building high-quality labeled datasets, offering automated labeling features to reduce annotation costs.
3. **Prodigy:**
- o URL: https://prodi.gy

○   Description: Annotation tool designed for NLP tasks, supporting active learning workflows to improve annotation efficiency.

APPENDIX D: ETHICAL GUIDELINES AND FRAMEWORKS

AI Ethics Guidelines by the European Commission:

- URL: https://ec.europa.eu/digital-strategy
- Description: Guidelines focusing on ensuring AI is ethical, fair, and respects fundamental rights, with principles on transparency, accountability, and privacy.

IEEE's Ethically Aligned Design:

- URL: https://ethicsinaction.ieee.org
- Description: Frameworks and guidelines for ethical AI development, emphasizing human rights, well-being, accountability, and transparency.

Partnership on AI:

- URL: https://www.partnershiponai.org
- Description: Multi-stakeholder organization developing best practices for AI, addressing fairness, transparency, and inclusivity in AI systems.

CONCLUSION

This comprehensive guide has provided an in-depth exploration of prompt engineering, covering foundational concepts, advanced techniques, practical applications, and ethical considerations. By following the principles and strategies outlined in this guide, practitioners can master the art and science of prompt engineering, creating effective, ethical, and innovative AI systems that drive positive impact across various domains. As the field continues to evolve, staying informed and engaged with the latest developments and best practices will be essential for continued success and innovation in prompt engineering.

This completes the comprehensive guide on prompt engineering. We hope this resource serves as a valuable reference for your ongoing journey in mastering prompt engineering and leveraging its full potential in AI-driven interactions. Thank you for exploring this field with us.

www.ingramcontent.com/pod-product-compliance
Lightning Source LLC
LaVergne TN
LVHW051432050326
832903LV00030BD/3051